O Come Let Us
ADORE HIM

31 CHRISTMAS DEVOTIONALS TO FIND MEANING IN THE MANGER

ROB LONG

Copyright © 2023 by Rob Long

All rights reserved. This book or any portion thereof may not be reproduced or used in any manner whatsoever without the express written permission of the publisher except for the use of brief quotations in a book review or scholarly journal.

First Printing: 2023

All Scripture quotations, unless otherwise indicated, are taken from the Holy Bible, New International Version®, NIV®. Copyright © 1973, 1978, 1984, 2011 by Biblica, Inc.™ Used by permission of Zondervan. All rights reserved worldwide. www.zondervan.com The "NIV" and "New International Version" are trademarks registered in the United States Patent and Trademark Office by Biblica, Inc.™

ISBN-13: 979-8-8603967-2-2

Praise for
O Come Let Us Adore Him

"Readers of *O Come Let Us Adore Him* are repeatedly invited to fix their eyes on Jesus and experience the worship, adoration, and transformation that inevitably follows. Long expertly weaves Scripture, stories, and reflection to inspire a spirit of worship as well as a conviction to be transformed more into the image of Christ. Make this book an annual holiday tradition."
- **Jeremy Robertson**, Youth & Family Minister, Edmond Church of Christ

"*O Come Let Us Adore Him* is a beautiful place of quiet rest to slow down and reflect on God's promises to us--promises that see their fullness in the incarnation of Jesus Christ. Each day's reading provides insight into the Word, meaningful reflection, and most significantly, hope of an ever-present Savior in a broken world. I can't wait for my family to share in these daily devotionals as we celebrate Advent this year."
- **Danny Camp**, Counselor, Agape Nashville

"Each Christmas season it is more and more challenging as followers of Christ to sift through the commercialism and materialism of "Today's Christmas" and experience the "salvation now out in the open for everyone to see" that Simeon spoke of in Luke 2. Rob Long does a wonderful job of bringing the reader, congregation, or family to better know and recognize Jesus Christ and that salvation. *O Come Let Us Adore Him* had me laughing at times and crying at times but throughout it had me grappling with my faith and with scripture in a way that was both refreshing and enlightening. This is one for all disciples to integrate into each and every Christmas season!"
- **Kelly Tomasi**, College Minister, Bulldogs for Christ and Weatherford Church of Christ, Weatherford, OK

"2000 years ago, angels came and announced, "Behold I bring you good news of great joy" (Luke 2:10). God gave the world the gift of Jesus and that gift changed everything. In this timely work, Rob Long skillfully and passionately reminds us of the good news of Jesus' coming and the great joy we can experience when we fully receive that gift. Read it. Soak it up. Be blessed!"
  - **Johnny Markham**, Family/Executive Minister, College Hills Church of Christ

"Do you wish your kids had a deeper connection to Christmas than just the presents on their wish list? Spend just a few minutes each day this December with your family and this devotional book and they will experience and understand what Christmas is truly about in a new and meaningful way."
  - **Seth McDowell**, Senior Minister, Shawnee Trail Church of Christ

"In *O Come Let Us Adore Him* Rob Long demonstrates a unique grasp of scripture, and personal relationship with God to remind readers of the transforming power of the birth of Jesus."
  - **Jamie Riley**, Family Life Minister, Sunshine Church of Christ

"Rob Long has written a Christmas devotional which chronicles the Savior's birth that motivates and inspires the reader to worship and adore Him! A must read."
  - **Patrick Johnson**, Senior Evangelist, Peyton Road Church of Christ

To Sarah, Adelyn, and Audrey.

After Jesus, you three are the best gift.

Table of Contents

	Foreword	i
	Introduction	1
December 1	Glory in a Feed Trough	3
December 2	He Came to Save	7
December 3	KYAL	12
December 4	The Invisible Made Visible	16
December 5	You are Rich	21
December 6	Broken, Yet Beautiful	27
December 7	Divine Interruptions	33
December 8	Shining Brightly for ALL to See	38
December 9	"The Heart is Everything"	43
December 10	God *With* Us	48
December 11	He Gets Us	53
December 12	A Gift Fit for a King	58
December 13	Waiting and Watching	64
December 14	"Who Among Us Will Celebrate Christmas Right?"	69
December 15	Satan's Perspective on Christmas	73
December 16	Trusting God Through Disappointment	78

December 17	The Lord's Servant	83
December 18	Blessed is She Who Has Believed	88
December 19	The World Turned Upside Down	93
December 20	Greatness in the Manger	98
December 21	Hope in the Manger	103
December 22	Joy in the Manger	108
December 23	The Gift in the Manger	113
December 24	Peace in the Manger	118
December 25	Love in the Manger	123
December 26	Christ Born in Us	129
December 27	Christ in Us: His Faithfulness	134
December 28	Christ in Us: His Compassion	139
December 29	Christ in Us: His Service	144
December 30	Christ in Us: His Surrender	149
December 31	Christ in Us: His Grace	154
	Acknowledgements	158
	Bibliography	159
	About the Author	161

"Christmas and the incarnation mean that God went to infinite lengths to make himself one whom we can know personally."

- Timothy Keller

Foreword

As I write these words, the place where the Prince of Peace was born is at war. Bombs are being dropped, shots are being fired and families are torn apart. The land where our Savior first took air into His human lungs is now filled with smoke. The message of "peace on earth" seems to be forgotten.

Rob Long has written words that can help bring you peace this holiday season. He brings the Savior of the stable into our modern context. Rob reminds us that the peace that was promised centuries before the miracle in Bethlehem is still as relevant today as it was the moment the Spirit breathed it.

Peace is but one aspect you will discover in the pages of this book. You will also find hope, and love, and forgiveness. Jesus is not to be left in the manger. He is not left hanging on the cross. He is alive! Equally important, He is relevant to whatever place you find yourself in this season of life.

Whatever your problems, whatever your issues, they are not too big for the Savior born in Bethlehem. Jesus overcame poverty, disappointment, abandonment and many other struggles with which we wrestle.

Join me in recommitting to worshipping the King of Kings. Don't just read the words as you drink your coffee and enjoy your devotional time. Let these thoughts from Rob penetrate deep into your soul. Spend each day throughout the holidays bringing your family and friends to the manger, to the cross, to the empty tomb, in order to proclaim, "O Come Let Us Adore Him."

Dr. David Duncan, Preaching Minister
Memorial Church of Christ, Houston, TX

INTRODUCTION

It was a bitterly cold December night in Northwest Ohio. In a church bus-turned-sleigh, about ten of us ventured through Toledo to deliver Christmas gifts to children in need. As the evening went on, I noted that our mission took us into areas of Toledo I had been cautioned to avoid. We were on the "other side of the tracks." At each new stop, Santa and his helpers did what they do best – brought joy to children. While Santa showered the kids with gifts and Christmas cheer, I glanced at the parents, hoping they would not feel embarrassed by our presence and charity. Thankfully, that is not what I observed. Instead, I noticed looks of appreciation and excitement, undoubtedly prompted by the sparkle in their children's eyes. An almost palpable contrast existed between the cold, dark night outside and the warmth and light inside where the joy of Christmas filled the air.

That night I witnessed the tangible impact Christians can make when they choose to be the hands and feet of Jesus. The transcendent glow filling each of those homes was, I believe, the light of Christ shining through His followers. Regardless of what those children and their parents had endured, in that moment, it was clear that the love and light of Jesus brought them a glimmer of hope and peace.

2000 years ago, God gave the world a gift that changed everything. The angel announced, "Today in the town of David a Savior has been born to you; he is the Messiah, the Lord" (Luke 2:11). Just as God's love and light invaded those Toledo homes in the presence of Santa Claus, God's love and light invaded the earth when Jesus was born in a Bethlehem stable. God ventured to the "other side of the tracks." John said, "In him was life, and that life was the light of all mankind" (John 1:4). Jesus is the greatest gift the world has ever beheld. Without Jesus, all of humanity would be lost, alone, dead, and left in the dark. God made a move before any of us even knew what we needed. He sent His Son as the perfect gift to be our King and Savior; not because we deserve this gift, but because He loves us that much (John 3:16-17). That is the main message of the manger.

How can we embrace this abiding truth amid life's busyness? December can feel chaotic with the parties, shopping, school activities, and projects that fill the holiday season. These devotionals are an invitation to stop for a few minutes each day and dwell with the Word of God, especially around the topic of Jesus' birth, so that you can remain grounded in the Truth.

What difference does the Incarnation make in our everyday lives… throughout the past year, during the present season, and in the upcoming year?

As you embark on this journey, I pray that God will give you the eyes to see what He wants to reveal as you gaze at the one born in the town of David.

O come, let us adore him,
O come, let us adore him,
O come, let us adore him,
Christ the Lord.

December 1

Glory in a Feed Trough

"May God give you peace with yourselves; may He give you good will towards all your friends, your enemies, and your neighbors; and may He give you grace to give glory to God in the highest."

- C.H. Spurgeon

O Come Let Us ADORE HIM

TODAY'S SCRIPTURE

In the beginning was the Word, and the Word was with God, and the Word was God. He was with God in the beginning. The Word became flesh and made his dwelling among us. We have seen his glory, the glory of the one and only Son, who came from the Father, full of grace and truth.

JOHN 1:1-2, 14

REFLECTION

God showed up in a feed trough.

The Messiah's birth was more *Little House on the Prairie* than *Downton Abbey*. He was not born in a palace as you might expect for royalty, but in an animal shelter with a feed trough as His bed. As Mary gently cared for her newborn baby, smells of manure, woodchips, and dirt filled the room. Sounds of cows chomping on their food, sheep bleating aimlessly, and townspeople bustling about before daybreak echoed in the background. Picture this young mother tenderly consoling the infant-God as his tiny cheek pressed against her shoulder and neck, all the while surrounded by dirty sheep, donkeys, and oxen. God enters the world like this.

This kind of Messianic entrance is surely not what the Jewish people expected. What they anticipated resembled what they knew of the mighty King Solomon. Solomon, the famous king of Israel, was "greater in riches" than all the other kings of the earth. His days in power were the glory days of Israel. In those days, they stood on top of the world.

Solomon was enormously wealthy. We read about him: "The king made a throne covered with ivory and overlaid with pure gold. The throne had six steps, and a footstool of gold was attached to it. . . All King Solomon's goblets were gold, and all the household articles in the Palace of the Forest of Lebanon were pure gold" (2 Chronicles 9:13-20). With Solomon's gold-covered palace in mind, the Jewish people likely reminisced about him when the prophets spoke of the coming Messiah.

Perhaps they thought, 'Get ready, goldsmiths, because you're about to get really busy... here comes the Messiah!'

But in a mammoth plot twist, the Messiah showed up not in a gold-plated palace, but in a dirt-filled stable. Philip Yancey commented, "The God who roared, who could order armies and empires about like pawns on a chessboard, this God emerged in Palestine as a baby who could not speak or eat solid food or control his bladder, who depended on a teenage couple for food, shelter, and love."

Peering into the stable, seeing the feed trough, imagining the smells and the sounds reminds us that God does not need exquisite goblets or a golden throne to radiate His glorious presence. The full weight of His glory came amid the smells, sounds, and sights of the stable.

The Creator of the world became a fetus with tiny organs, limbs, bones, muscles, and facial features developing within Mary's womb. The Creator became the creation. He was fed, comforted, cleaned up, and rocked. In God coming near, His glory was visible up close and personal.

In most world religions, followers must strain and struggle to achieve closeness to a god or deity. In Christianity, however, God came to us. He closed the gap by entering our world and revealing His glory right in the middle of everyday life. This Christmas, I encourage you to step into the stable and observe the delivery room of the Son of God. Meditate on what you smell, see, and hear. Then, reflect on what the manner of Jesus' birth teaches you about God.

If God's glory can appear in an animal stall in Bethlehem, it can appear anywhere. So, keep your eyes open for His glory today!

O Come Let Us ADORE HIM

QUESTIONS

1) What do you hope to achieve by working through this month-long Christmas devotional?
2) In the last year, how have you seen the glory of God most clearly? What stands out to you about each of those moments?

PRAYER

Father, thank you for revealing who you are to us through your Son born in Bethlehem. That your glory filled a dingy animal stall in the backwoods community of Bethlehem shows you can reveal your glory anywhere. Give me eyes to see your glory radiating all around me. Also, as I embark on this month-long journey of reflection on Jesus' birth, prepare my heart to create room for Him so that He can reign within me forever as my King…all to your glory! Amen.

December 2

He Came to Save

"Christmas is God lighting a candle; and you don't light a candle in a room that's already full of sunlight. You light a candle in a room that's so murky that the candle, when lit, reveals just how bad things really are."

- N. T. Wright

O Come Let Us ADORE HIM

TODAY'S SCRIPTURES

This is how the birth of Jesus the Messiah came about: His mother Mary was pledged to be married to Joseph, but before they came together, she was found to be pregnant through the Holy Spirit. Because Joseph her husband was faithful to the law, and yet did not want to expose her to public disgrace, he had in mind to divorce her quietly. But after he had considered this, an angel of the Lord appeared to him in a dream and said, "Joseph son of David, do not be afraid to take Mary home as your wife, because what is conceived in her is from the Holy Spirit. She will give birth to a son, and you are to give him the name Jesus, because he will save his people from their sins."

MATTHEW 1:18-21

For the wages of sin is death, but the gift of God is eternal life in Christ Jesus our Lord.

ROMANS 6:23

REFLECTION

Jesus saves.

Once, while visiting South Carolina, my wife Sarah and I decided on a whim to attend a Christian music concert. There was a woman in front of us who caught our attention. She stood most of the concert. At one point, she held her little daughter in one arm while lifting the other arm above her head in praise. To be honest, I was nervous she was going to drop her baby! But what really struck me were her tears. I could be wrong, but I think she was carrying a heavy load that night and needed an encounter with her Savior.

God gave His Son the name Jesus because "he will save his people from their sins" (Matthew 1:21). "Jesus" is literally Yeshua, or Joshua, which means "God is deliverance." Jesus arrived to save us from our sins and its consequences.

Sin is at the core of all the problems in the world – whether on a small scale or even globally – because it separates us from God. From the moment Adam and Eve disobeyed God in the garden by eating the forbidden fruit, sin has infected our world. It's a problem for us all.

In today's culture, talking about sin is out of style. Maybe it's too negative, condescending, or narrow-minded to do so. But if we dismiss the problem of sin, we dismiss God's solution to fix it. What's the use of a Savior if there's nothing to be saved from? On an individual level, things like self-help books, personality assessments, and counseling all have their place (I have been helped tremendously by each), but none of them can do for us what Jesus can do. He is the only solution to our sin problem. He is the Savior. Paul said, "For the wages of sin is death, but the gift of God is eternal life in Christ Jesus our Lord" (Romans 6:23).

The baby in the manger grew up to become a mature man. While remaining as sinless as the day He was born, He was unjustly killed. It was a monumental sacrifice even for Jesus to let go of His heavenly splendor and live as a human with all the trials and struggles involved in this earthly life. So, for Jesus to leave heaven to die a cruel, shameful, humiliating death, in addition to experiencing all that is involved in being a human being, is almost beyond comprehension.

Consider this: While suffering on the Cross, Jesus made that heart-wrenching statement: "My God, my God, why have you forsaken me" (Matthew 27:46)? In deep anguish, Jesus was forsaken by his Father as He bore our sins. He abandoned the peace and beauty of heaven to experience the pain of earth in the ugliest, most humiliating and gruesome way so that we could one day experience the peace and beauty of heaven ourselves in the future.

As you gaze into the manger this Christmas, see the baby Savior who would one day die the death you deserve so that you can be saved. God traveled an infinite distance, in love, to give you this gift. I think the woman at the South Carolina concert understood how special the gift of Jesus truly was, which is why she worshiped with holy expectation.

Timothy Keller wrote in his book *Hidden Christmas,* "There has never been a gift offered that makes you swallow your pride

O Come Let Us ADORE HIM

to the depths that the gift of Jesus Christ requires us to do. Christmas means that we are so lost, so unable to save ourselves, that nothing less than the death of the Son of God himself could save us."

Jesus really is the best gift because He saves.

If sin, shame, and guilt continue to load you down, remember Jesus saves. Embrace His deliverance today.

QUESTIONS

1) Are there any sins you have been carrying that you need to confess to God today to experience his forgiveness and healing?
2) Have you been taking for granted the amazing gift of Jesus in your life? Do you long for a special encounter with God like the woman at the concert?

PRAYER

Father, thank you for sending the Savior to the world. Help me to understand today how amazing and needed your gift of Jesus truly was. I would be lost in sin and death, held in Satan's grip, if it were not for my Savior, Jesus Christ. I want to live today in such a way that my gratitude for that gift is evident in everything I say and do. In Jesus' name, amen.

DECEMBER 3

KYAL

"God with us, Immanuel, driving out fear with good news, driving out the questions of "Am I good enough? Can I be loved? Do I matter?" Driving out the fear with his love, showing up and in all power and might reordering our affections so that "Glory to God in the highest" becomes our mantra. Then from there we see this profound sense of God's desire to pull in from the least of these those He will call sons and daughters."

- MATT CHANDLER

O Come Let Us **ADORE HIM**

TODAY'S SCRIPTURES

For God so loved the world that he gave his one and only Son, that whoever believes in him shall not perish but have eternal life.

JOHN 3:16

Dear friends, let us love one another, for love comes from God. Everyone who loves has been born of God and knows God. Whoever does not love does not know God, because God is love. This is how God showed his love among us: He sent his one and only Son into the world that we might live through him.

1 JOHN 4:7-9

REFLECTION

KYAL. For years, my friend DJ has included these four letters at the end of his social media posts. KYAL stands for "know you are loved." I appreciate his desire to communicate this message consistently in a creative way. And DJ is one of those people who wants every person he encounters to know they are loved. He is a genuinely loving person. I wish I were more like him in that way.

"Know you are loved" is such an important message because many of us struggle to believe it. Symptoms of the belief that we are not loved include feeling alone, perpetually sad, or like we do not measure up. These emotions are commonly accompanied by shame and guilt. Sometimes as we struggle to process these feelings in a healthy way, we seek to numb them, bury them, or ignore them, hoping they will not hurt as much.

Christmas can feel, in a word, heavy. Sometimes "the most wonderful time of the year" isn't exactly wonderful. December brings out people's stress, anxiety, exhaustion, and a heightened burnout level, making it feel like we are on the brink of a meltdown. Some of us try to fool ourselves into thinking next December will be better... more peaceful. Ironically, a season designed to celebrate the birth of a loving Savior can cause people to act very unloving toward each other.

O Come Let Us ADORE HIM

All this unloveliness surely breaks God's heart. Especially when you consider that, in love, He sent his Son to earth as a human. Jesus stood in the crosshairs of the world's unloveliness and was maligned, rejected, denied, and eventually killed. He endured humanity's worst, so humanity could see true love at its best. All you have to do is look at the cross: KYAL.

Today if you feel unloved and overlooked, be assured you are not. That is a lie. The truth is that you are unbelievably loved. Through the manger, the cross, and the empty tomb God expresses his deep, eternal love for you.

I encourage you to pray this prayer written by Henri Nouwen:

"O Lord, how hard it is to accept your way. You come to me as a small, powerless child born away from home. You live for me as a stranger in your own land. You die for me as a criminal outside the walls of the city, rejected by your own people, misunderstood by your friends, and feeling abandoned by your God.

As I prepare to celebrate your birth, I am trying to feel loved, accepted, and at home in this world, and I am trying to overcome the feelings of alienation and separation which continue to assail me. But I wonder now if my deep sense of homelessness does not bring me closer to you than my occasional feelings of belonging. Where do I truly celebrate your birth: in a cozy home or in an unfamiliar house, among welcoming friends or among unknown strangers, with feelings of well-being or with feelings of loneliness?

I do not have to run away from those experiences that are closest to yours. Just as you do not belong to this world, so I do not belong to this world. Every time I feel this way I have an occasion to be grateful and to embrace you better and taste more fully your joy and peace.

Come, Lord Jesus, and be with me where I feel poorest. I trust that this is the place where you will find your manger and bring your light. Come, Lord Jesus, come."

KYAL.

O Come Let Us **ADORE HIM**

QUESTIONS

1) How does reflecting on Jesus' birth, ministry, death, and resurrection impact how you understand God's love?
2) Do you know someone who needs to hear KYAL today? How will you communicate that message to them?

PRAYER

God, thank you for loving me enough to send your Son as my Savior and King. Knowing Jesus helps me understand that you deeply love me. Use me to be an instrument of your love toward others. If at times I don't feel loved, please send me reminders to show me, again, the depth of your love for me. In Jesus' name, amen.

December 4

The Invisible Made Visible

"The birth of Jesus is a birth with a message. It takes the entire Bible to bring the complete message, but this birth is the core of it: In Jesus, God is here to give us life, real life."

- Eugene Peterson

O Come Let Us ADORE HIM

TODAY'S SCRIPTURES

In the past God spoke to our ancestors through the prophets at many times and in various ways, but in these last days he has spoken to us by his Son, whom he appointed heir of all things, and through whom also he made the universe. The Son is the radiance of God's glory and the exact representation of his being, sustaining all things by his powerful word.

HEBREWS 1:1-3

In the beginning was the Word, and the Word was with God, and the Word was God. He was with God in the beginning. Through him all things were made; without him nothing was made that has been made. The Word became flesh and made his dwelling among us. We have seen his glory, the glory of the one and only Son, who came from the Father, full of grace and truth. (John testified concerning him. He cried out, saying, "This is the one I spoke about when I said, 'He who comes after me has surpassed me because he was before me.'") Out of his fullness we have all received grace in place of grace already given. For the law was given through Moses; grace and truth came through Jesus Christ. No one has ever seen God, but the one and only Son, who is himself God and is in closest relationship with the Father, has made him known.

JOHN 1:1, 14-18

The Son is the image of the invisible God, the firstborn over all creation.

COLOSSIANS 1:15

REFLECTION

Bethlehem reminds us that God revealed Himself most fully by sending His Son, not a letter, constitution, statue, or museum. The biblical writers use different language to make this singular point. Regarding Jesus, the writer of Hebrews said He is "the exact representation" of God's being; John wrote that the Word "was God"; and Paul added, "The Son is the image of the invisible God." Therefore, we must know the Son. When we see the Son, we see God.

O Come Let Us ADORE HIM

Imagine learning to play tennis. The first thing you do is schedule a lesson with a new coach. On the afternoon of your first practice, you arrive with racket in hand, ready to learn. As you step onto the court, you see no one. The place is empty. After a few minutes, your coach sends a text message. Strangely, the message contains a few bullet points on tennis fundamentals. The coach concludes the message by saying that if you follow his plan, you will master the game. "No face-to-face instruction is necessary; you will be learning the game over text messages." Disappointed, you immediately begin your search for a new coach.

Now, a different scenario. You show up for your first tennis lesson. As you step onto the court, you notice that someone has arrived before you. To your surprise, it is Rafael Nadal, one of the greatest players ever. You are shocked that today you will be sharing a court with tennis greatness. His presence puzzles you. Then he approaches you and says, "Hello, I'm your new tennis coach." Of course, he intimidates you, but he quickly reassures you that he will be patient. He is committed to being your tennis coach... for life. Your new teacher is one of the best of all time.

The second scenario illustrates what God has done through Jesus. God sent His Son to show us how to live. Our teacher is the best of all time. In Jesus, the invisible God became visible.

While in the Old Testament, God made only a few appearances (burning bush, cloud, pillar of fire), in Jesus, God put on skin so that all could see Him, touch Him, and learn from Him. The Word of God, Jesus Christ, befriended sinners; called tax collectors to follow him, stood up for the sinful woman caught in adultery, welcomed children to his embrace, and forgave the ones who crucified Him. Through His interactions, Jesus revealed the Father to the world. Do you want to know what God is like and what He desires? Look to Jesus.

Learning from, and following, Jesus happens in a myriad of ways, such as: reading the Gospels, fellowshipping with other Christians, gathering for communion with the church, serving the poor, and living under the guidance of the Holy Spirit. Therefore, we should make these a fixture in our lives. Step by step, we learn about God from our teacher, Jesus.

My friend, Colton, often uses an illustration involving Lebron James. He says, "I may tell someone I know Lebron James. But is Lebron my friend? I mean, I've watched him a ton on TV and been amazed at his abilities. But, if Lebron saw me at the store would he know who I am? Do I really *know* Lebron James? I know *about* Lebron James, but I don't have a relationship with him." Then he brings the point home by saying, "Do I really know Jesus? Not just, do I know *about* Jesus? But, do I truly *know* Jesus? Do I have a relationship with Him – does He know who I am, and do I know Him? Most importantly, have I spent *time* with Jesus to truly know Him?" Colton's point is clear: our desire should exceed merely knowing *about* Jesus, as if He is a celebrity on TV; we should strive to know Him personally, which requires effort and intentionality.

As you continue this month-long journey of reflection on Jesus' birth, I encourage you to ask God to give you eyes to see Jesus, a mind ready to learn from Him, hands to serve Him, and feet to follow Him. I pray that you will make the effort to truly *know* Jesus, not just *about* Him.

O Come Let Us ADORE HIM

QUESTIONS

1) How can you prepare your heart and mind to see Jesus today?
2) What are some things in life that act as blinders to seeing Jesus? What steps can you take to remove those blinders?
3) How has seeing and knowing Jesus helped you understand and appreciate God more fully?

PRAYER

Father, thank you for revealing fully who you are through your Son, Jesus. You have not left me alone or without direction on how to live. Give me eyes to see your Son, so that I can not only see Him, but you, too. If there is pride, apathy, or confusion in my heart, please remove it so that my heart can be fully yours. Help me to know Jesus personally and closely. In His holy name, amen.

December 5

You are Rich

"Whoever finds Jesus, finds a rich treasure, and a good above every good. He who loses Jesus loses much indeed, and more than the whole world. Poorest of all is he who lives without Jesus, and richest of all is he who stands in favor with Jesus."

- Thomas a Kempis

O Come Let Us ADORE HIM

TODAY'S SCRIPTURES

For you know the grace of our Lord Jesus Christ, that though he was rich, yet for your sake he became poor, so that you through his poverty might become rich.

2 CORINTHIANS 8:9

In your relationships with one another, have the same mindset as Christ Jesus:
  Who, being in very nature God,
  did not consider equality with God something to be used to his own advantage;
  rather, he made himself nothing
  by taking the very nature of a servant,
  being made in human likeness.
  And being found in appearance as a man,
  he humbled himself
  by becoming obedient to death—
  even death on a cross!

PHILIPPIANS 2:5-8

REFLECTION

In the classic movie *Planes, Trains, and Automobiles,* Del Griffith, played by John Candy, tells a hotel clerk that he's "still a million bucks shy of being a millionaire." Del Griffith apparently did not think he was rich. How about you? Are you rich?

You cannot argue with the fact that we live in a wealthy country. On Black Friday in 2022, Americans spent over nine billion dollars in online Christmas shopping according to USA Today. That is just online! Currently, American households hold close to $150 trillion dollars in wealth according to the Brookings Institute. The amount of wealth in our country is staggering. And if you have ever spent time in a different country, you have likely felt the enormity of America's wealth even more intensely. Each time I travel to Haiti, in particular, the stark contrast between the two countries overwhelms me.

But, of course, there is more to being rich than the size of your bank account, how much you spend on Amazon, the square footage of your house, the vacations you take, or the type of car you drive.

Paul wrote, "For you know the grace of our Lord Jesus Christ, that though he was rich, yet for your sake he became poor, so that you through his poverty might become rich" (2 Corinthians 8:9). Jesus arrived on earth, surrendering the splendor of heaven so that we can be rich. Some of the riches offered through Jesus include these amazing gifts: the Father's inheritance, the provision of our Almighty God, being part of the family of faith, and having a heavenly Father and Shepherd who will never leave us nor forsake us. Being a millionaire pales in comparison to the riches available to us by God through Christ.

Paul also wrote that Jesus, although "being in very nature God, did not consider equality with God something to be used for his own advantage; rather he made himself nothing...being made in human likeness" (Philippians 2:6-8). Jesus "made himself nothing" by letting go of his heavenly glories and comforts and choosing to become flesh and bone, experiencing life as a human being. He did not become 46% or 78% human, rather he became 100% human.

J.I. Packer wrote of Jesus' descent to earth: "It meant love to the uttermost for unlovely human beings, that they through his poverty might become rich. The Christmas message is that there is hope for a ruined humanity – hope of pardon, hope of peace with God, hope of glory-because at the Father's will Jesus Christ became poor and was born in a stable so that thirty years later he might hang on a cross. It is the most wonderful message that the world has ever heard or will hear."

Warning: The enemy wants you to focus on what you *don't have*. He would love for you to compare yourself to others and conclude that you do not measure up. He wants you to feel poor, insecure, destitute, and alone. He wants you to live with a scarcity mindset instead of an abundance mindset. Do not buy into the lies! Remember that God's children are the wealthiest people on the planet; we have everything we need. C.S. Lewis aptly stated, "He who has God and everything else has no more than he who has God only."

Jewish families, when celebrating Passover each year, re-tell the story of God's mighty acts through the Dayenu Prayer. Dayenu means "It would have been enough." The Jewish people incorporated this prayer into their Passover observance in the ninth century to acknowledge God's faithfulness toward, and provision for, their people. While we are not Jewish, the Dayenu Prayer can provide us rich language to express our gratitude to God for His constant provision.

> *If He had brought us out of Egypt, Dayenu ("It would have been enough")*
> *If He had executed justice upon the Egyptians, Dayenu*
> *If He had executed justice upon their gods, Dayenu*
> *If He had slain their first-born, Dayenu*
> *If He had given to us their health and wealth, Dayenu*
> *If He had split the sea for us, Dayenu*
> *If He had led us through on dry land, Dayenu*
> *If He had drowned our oppressors, Dayenu*
> *If He had provided for our needs in the wilderness for 40 years, Dayenu*
> *If He had fed us manna, Dayenu*
> *If He had given us Shabbat, Dayenu*
> *If He had led us to Mount Sinai, Dayenu*
> *If He had given us the Torah, Dayenu*
> *If He had brought us into the Land of Israel, Dayenu*
> *If He built the Temple for us, Dayenu ("It would have been enough")*

As you can see in the Dayenu Prayer, just one miracle would have been sufficient for the people; however, the song acknowledges how God's miracles flowed like a river providing hope, protection, and life for His people. Today, we can say the same thing. While God certainly does not owe us anything, His provisions persist. Just one act of generosity from God would have been enough, but His love and mercy flow into our lives like a mighty river.

God has blessed us beyond measure. This Christmas, you may be a few bucks short of being a millionaire, but if you are a Christian, you are indeed the richest person on the planet because your treasure is Jesus himself.

O Come Let Us **ADORE HIM**

QUESTIONS

1) How can knowing "you are the richest person on the planet" in Christ change your perspective on life?
2) What is one specific way you can exercise generosity today to bless someone else?
3) Considering all the ways God has cared for you, especially in the gift of Jesus, how might you cultivate contentment in your life?

PRAYER

Father, I will be forever grateful for Jesus' willingness to empty Himself by becoming a man and ultimately dying the death I deserved. He is my treasure. Thank you for making me spiritually rich through Him. Please correct me by the guidance of the Holy Spirit when I forget the price He paid for me so that I can have an abundance of treasures through Him. Empower me to face this day with the mindset that I am rich in you. In Jesus' name, amen.

December 6

Broken, Yet Beautiful

"I used to think you had to be special for God to use you, but now I know you simply need to say 'yes.'"

- Bob Goff

O Come Let Us ADORE HIM

TODAY'S SCRIPTURE

This is the genealogy of Jesus the Messiah the son of David, the son of Abraham:
Abraham was the father of Isaac,
Isaac the father of Jacob,
Jacob the father of Judah and his brothers,
Judah the father of Perez and Zerah, whose mother was Tamar,
Perez the father of Hezron,
Hezron the father of Ram,
Ram the father of Amminadab,
Amminadab the father of Nahshon,
Nahshon the father of Salmon,
Salmon the father of Boaz, whose mother was Rahab,
Boaz the father of Obed, whose mother was Ruth,
Obed the father of Jesse,
and Jesse the father of King David.
David was the father of Solomon, whose mother had been Uriah's wife,
Solomon the father of Rehoboam,
Rehoboam the father of Abijah,
Abijah the father of Asa,
Asa the father of Jehoshaphat,
Jehoshaphat the father of Jehoram,
Jehoram the father of Uzziah,
Uzziah the father of Jotham,
Jotham the father of Ahaz,
Ahaz the father of Hezekiah,
Hezekiah the father of Manasseh,
Manasseh the father of Amon,
Amon the father of Josiah,
and Josiah the father of Jeconiah and his brothers at the time of the exile to Babylon.
After the exile to Babylon:
Jeconiah was the father of Shealtiel,
Shealtiel the father of Zerubbabel,
Zerubbabel the father of Abihud,
Abihud the father of Eliakim,

O Come Let Us ADORE HIM

Eliakim the father of Azor,
Azor the father of Zadok,
Zadok the father of Akim,
Akim the father of Elihud,
Elihud the father of Eleazar,
Eleazar the father of Matthan,
Matthan the father of Jacob,
and Jacob the father of Joseph, the husband of Mary, and Mary was the mother of Jesus who is called the Messiah.
Thus there were fourteen generations in all from Abraham to David, fourteen from David to the exile to Babylon, and fourteen from the exile to the Messiah.

MATTHEW 1:1-17

REFLECTION

Prior to telling us about Jesus' birth, Matthew gives us an extensive list of names, which seems like a strange way to start. Could you not produce a more exciting introduction, Matthew? However, upon closer look, this list perfectly introduces Matthew's central character. The genealogy traces Jesus' lineage back to both Abraham, the father of the Jews, and King David, which fulfills the Old Testament prophecies concerning the Messiah coming from David's line (Isaiah 7:14; 11:1-5). Beginning this way is Matthew's first evidence that Jesus is the true Messiah, and for a predominately Jewish audience, this family heritage is a non-negotiable for their King.

The genealogy consists of forty-six people spanning over two thousand years. The list includes well-known heroes such as Abraham, Isaac, Jacob, and David. Also included are lesser-known people, like Jothan, Zadok, and Akim; even a couple of shameless troublemakers - Manasseh and Abijah. The people on this list prove that God's mission was not compromised by the sins and failures of humans. It also demonstrates how God graciously works through ordinary people.

Notice four names: Tamar (an exploited mistress), Ruth (a non-Jew), Rahab (a prostitute), and Bathsheba (wronged by a king who abused his power). To a Jewish audience, the list's inclusion of women would have been a surprise because ancient genealogies were typically patriarchal in nature. Women in the first century were commonly overlooked, ignored, and even treated as property within the male-dominated ancient Middle Eastern culture. However, these unexpected individuals are noted for their role in bringing Jesus to the world.

And Jesus' mother, Mary, would join these four women in contributing to the Messiah's arrival. Acknowledging Jesus' female ancestors reminds us that while Mary's pregnancy may indeed appear scandalous, she is part of a heritage of mothers who dealt with their own scrutiny and public shame yet raised children who were blessed to fulfill God's purposes in the world.

Jesus' genealogy proves that God uses ordinary and broken people to accomplish His will. People like my friend Chris. For over fifteen years of his life, Chris was a drug addict, well-schooled in street life and violence. At age 35, he broke his neck jumping off a roof "amidst a cloud of narcotics." At that point, he entered a recovery program with the Salvation Army. In recovery, God revealed himself to Chris and caused him to see the darkness of his own sin. Chris surrendered to Jesus and began a journey of spiritual healing. As God healed him, Chris said "life became worth living, even beautiful."

Chris then worked for several different treatment centers to help people who fought similar battles. While working in those treatment facilities, Chris saw a troubling pattern. He noticed that after being discharged from a recovery program, a gap formed in a person's life. Without the support of a treatment facility, people became lonely and vulnerable, which made them susceptible to returning to the behaviors that led to their need for recovery in the first place.

So, Chris started an organization called The Gap to walk with people into the next chapter of their lives. He said, "It is our responsibility and my mission that no one, whether an addict or the loved one of an addict, has to go it alone. We stand in the gap with you." God is using Chris, a man who was on the brink of death, to change the lives of drug addicts and their families.

And here's the truth: If God can use Rahab, Ruth, Bathsheba, Tamar, Mary, or Chris to accomplish His mission in this world, He can use you.

O Come Let Us ADORE HIM

QUESTIONS

1) Do you know anyone who has experienced a transformation like Chris? If so, what did that transformation teach you about God?
2) Have you ever doubted that God can use you because of your past failures, inadequacies, or brokenness? How might the example of Ruth, Tamar, Bathsheba, and Rahab challenge your thinking?

PRAYER

Father, I learn so much about your grace and power from noticing the people you have used to accomplish your purposes in the world. If you can use Rahab, Ruth, Bathsheba, and Tamar to bring Jesus to this world, I know you can use me, too. While this world obsesses over personal achievement and self-promotion, keep me focused on serving you alone so that I can play my part in showing you to the world. I trust that you will accomplish wonderful things through me for your glory as I lay my life down before you. In Jesus' name, Amen.

December 7

Divine Interruptions

"Never be afraid to trust an unknown future to a known God."

- Corrie Ten Boom

O Come Let Us ADORE HIM

Today's Scripture

This is how the birth of Jesus the Messiah came about: His mother Mary was pledged to be married to Joseph, but before they came together, she was found to be pregnant through the Holy Spirit. Because Joseph her husband was faithful to the law, and yet did not want to expose her to public disgrace, he had in mind to divorce her quietly. But after he had considered this, an angel of the Lord appeared to him in a dream and said, "Joseph son of David, do not be afraid to take Mary home as your wife, because what is conceived in her is from the Holy Spirit. She will give birth to a son, and you are to give him the name Jesus, because he will save his people from their sins."
All this took place to fulfill what the Lord had said through the prophet: "The virgin will conceive and give birth to a son, and they will call him Immanuel" (which means "God with us").
When Joseph woke up, he did what the angel of the Lord had commanded him and took Mary home as his wife. ²⁵ *But he did not consummate their marriage until she gave birth to a son. And he gave him the name Jesus.*

MATTHEW 1:18-24

Reflection

A few years ago, an interview on BBC went viral because it captured a distinguished professor in a very human moment. While the professor offered his expert analysis on foreign policy during the live video feed, his young daughter sauntered into the room. Seconds later, another child entered in a baby walker. The first child approached her dad and positioned herself right next to him for the world to see. As this happened, the mother was in the background frantically trying to escort the little invaders out. Of course, the dad's embarrassment was all over his face.

This interview has been viewed over 56 million times on YouTube - not because of the impressive answers the professor provided, but because he was interrupted in a serious moment. I know if I were in his shoes, I would have been frustrated and embarrassed. I bet that office door has now been equipped with a lock and that the dad double-checks the children's whereabouts before the camera starts rolling.

Interruptions frustrate us. We have things to do, schedules to keep, places to be. The last thing we need is a wrench thrown into our day. 'Ain't nobody got time for that!'

Speaking of interruptions, consider the wrench thrown into Joseph's life. Upon learning of Mary's pregnancy, Joseph must have been torn to pieces, as the only logical explanation for Mary's pregnancy was adultery. Therefore, Joseph planned to divorce Mary quietly to protect her from "public disgrace." (In ancient Judaism, engagement was a legally binding commitment; also, Jewish tradition required divorce when adultery was involved). Despite being gutted, Joseph took the compassionate route with Mary so she would not be publicly shamed. Joseph's treatment of Mary revealed his character; he refused to seek revenge. He was a good man.

But then the angel told Joseph to marry his fiancée. She had not been unfaithful; in fact, she displayed great faith. The angel told Joseph the baby was from the Holy Spirit and that he should name the boy Jesus because "he will save His people from their sins."

Jesus did not arrive to earth in one of those chutes you see at the bank drive through. Nor did he descend to earth like a skydiver parachuting to the ground. He did not teleport from heaven to earth like a sci-fi character appearing out of thin air. Instead, Jesus' arrival to earth involved human parents, Joseph and Mary. Sidenote: Do you think it bothered Joseph that Mary got a Christmas song, "Mary, Did You Know?" and he did not?

Joseph probably had questions running through his mind: What does it mean that the baby is from the Holy Spirit? Why me? Why Mary? Why us? What about my reputation? My future? My life? How am I supposed to raise the Savior of the world? What if the boy is no good with a hammer?

You cannot overstate the gravity of God's call to Joseph. What an interruption! In the snap of a finger, Joseph's life was turned upside down.

Like Joseph, our lives can change abruptly. We could be

O Come Let Us ADORE HIM

moving to the rhythms of daily life, comforted by our routines like a warm blanket, appreciating our predictable and manageable schedules, and, boom, an interruption. With the snap of a finger, everything turns messy, unpredictable, out of rhythm, and seemingly unmanageable. The doctor says, "cancer." The manager says, "We're going a different direction, so we're letting you go." God calls you to a different place or ministry, the finances are depleted, your spouse takes their last breath, the teacher sends a note home, someone rejects you. Your rhythm is disrupted. The wind is knocked out of you.

Although Joseph does not get a song, he does play a key role in Jesus' earthly life. In doing so, he shows what it looks like to "Trust in the Lord with all your heart and lean not on your own understanding" (Proverbs 3:5). The interruption became the place to show that he trusted in the Lord. And the Lord was immensely faithful in return.

This Christmas season, consider Joseph's role in bringing Jesus to this world. Notice how he handled this seismic "interruption" in his young life. Notice how the "interruption" became an opportunity to play a part in God's salvation plan.

There is a valuable lesson here: Cling to God even in the interruption. You never know, God may use the interruption to teach you a lesson or to prepare you for something better than you could have ever imagined.

QUESTIONS

1) Try to put yourself in Joseph's shoes. What are some of the ways his life would have changed because of his role as Jesus' earthly father?
2) What have been some "interruptions" you have experienced in life? What have you learned from those interruptions?
3) As you look back at the last year, what specific situations have helped your trust grow the most?

PRAYER

Father, thank you for preserving your Word so that I can read about servants like Joseph. His example of handling a major "interruption" in his life inspires me to trust you and to not lean on my own understanding. I know you, God, so through life's many unknowns I can trust that everything will work out for good. Because you are good and faithful. In Jesus' name, amen.

DECEMBER 8

SHINING BRIGHTLY FOR ALL TO SEE

"Don't shine so others can see you. Shine so that through you others can see Him."

- C.S. LEWIS

O Come Let Us **ADORE HIM**

TODAY'S SCRIPTURE

After Jesus was born in Bethlehem in Judea, during the time of King Herod, Magi from the east came to Jerusalem and asked, "Where is the one who has been born king of the Jews? We saw his star when it rose and have come to worship him."

When King Herod heard this he was disturbed, and all Jerusalem with him. When he had called together all the people's chief priests and teachers of the law, he asked them where the Messiah was to be born. "In Bethlehem in Judea," they replied, "for this is what the prophet has written:

"'But you, Bethlehem, in the land of Judah,
are by no means least among the rulers of Judah;
for out of you will come a ruler
who will shepherd my people Israel.'"

Then Herod called the Magi secretly and found out from them the exact time the star had appeared. He sent them to Bethlehem and said, "Go and search carefully for the child. As soon as you find him, report to me, so that I too may go and worship him."

After they had heard the king, they went on their way, and the star they had seen when it rose went ahead of them until it stopped over the place where the child was. When they saw the star, they were overjoyed. On coming to the house, they saw the child with his mother Mary, and they bowed down and worshiped him. Then they opened their treasures and presented him with gifts of gold, frankincense and myrrh. And having been warned in a dream not to go back to Herod, they returned to their country by another route.

MATTHEW 2:1-12

REFLECTION

You may recall singing these words in church: "*The blessed Gospel is for all, The Gospel is for all; Where sin has gone must go His grace: The Gospel is for all.*" The Magi's presence during Jesus' infancy shows that the gospel truly is for all. Even before Jesus could walk or talk, the truth expressed in that old hymn was being realized. Eugene Boring explains who the Magi were and

O Come Let Us ADORE HIM

why their visit is so interesting:

> "*Magi* is the transliteration of Greek *magoi*, which can also be translated "wise men," "astrologers," or, as in the only other New Testament occurrence (Acts 13:6, 8) "magician" or "sorcerer." The word has nothing to do with "kings" (which comes from the later application of Psalm 72:10-11 and Isaiah 60:3 to the Christmas story) but designates a priestly class of Persian or Babylonian experts in the occult, such as astrology or the interpretation of dreams. They represent pagans (Gentiles) who, though they do not have the special revelation of the Torah, come to Jerusalem following the light they have seen" ("Matthew" in *The New Interpreter's Bible*).

The Magi, attuned to the will of God, traveled a long distance to worship Jesus and give him precious gifts. They fixed their eyes on the star leading them to the way, truth, and life. They bowed before the infant-God, testifying to the expanding nature of the Messiah's reign. If King Jesus can capture the hearts of these first century Persian men, then who really is beyond the reach of the good news of the Messiah? The gospel is for all.

Notice the difference in the responses of the Magi and Herod. Herod, who lived in Jesus' backyard, wanted to kill him, while the Magi, from probably 900-plus miles away, wanted to worship Him. Herod's motivation was self-preservation and personal power. He felt threatened, insecure, and jealous. Conversely, the Magi were humble, hopeful, and honorable.

It is not an accident that Jesus' earthly life is bookended with these Magi coming to worship Him when He was a small child and Him saying to his disciples, "Go and make disciples of all nations," (Matthew 28:19) right before returning to the Father. From arrival to ascension, He showed that His mission was undoubtedly for all nations. The gospel is for all.

Further, think about how the Magi got to Jesus in the first place. A star caught their eye. Then, with eyes on the star, they journeyed to Jerusalem and eventually to Bethlehem. You cannot help but see a connection between the star the Magi saw and what Paul said of Christians in Philippians. Paul wrote, "Do everything without grumbling or arguing, so that you may become blameless and pure, 'children of God without fault in a warped and crooked generation.' **Then you will shine among them like stars in the sky**, as you hold firmly to the word of life" (Philippians 2:14-16a, emphasis added).

As Christians, we are to shine like stars leading people to Jesus as we "hold firmly to the word of life." I encourage you the next clear night to look up at the sky and take in the view. As you look up, ask yourself, "What does it mean to be like the stars shining in the evening sky?" One thing I know about stars is that even though they are an insanely long way from earth, they can be clearly seen because of their brightness. And, regardless of the night's darkness, the star's light breaks through it. Therefore, a star's beauty, brilliance, and brightness will capture the attention and appreciation of those willing to see.

With that in mind, remember:

Once, God used a star to capture the attention of the Magi to lead them to Jesus.

Today, God is still using stars to capture the attention of people to lead them to Jesus.

You are one of those stars shining brightly.

You never know who God may use you to lead to Jesus.

O Come Let Us ADORE HIM

QUESTIONS

1) Over the last year, who have you witnessed being a shining star? In what specific ways did they shine? What have you learned from their example?
2) What does "the Gospel is for all" mean to you? How does the Magi's response to Jesus prove that the gospel truly is for all?
3) In the next year, what are some ways you may be able to step out of your comfort zone to connect with people different than you? (i.e. serve in an inner-city mission, go on a foreign mission trip, serve in the schools, volunteer at a benevolent center)

PRAYER

Father, thank you for calling me out of darkness into your glorious light through your Son, Jesus. Shine through me so that others may be drawn to you. The Magi remind me that the Gospel truly is for all. Forgive me for the times I think there are people beyond the reach of your loving arms. I truly believe nothing is impossible with you. In Jesus' name, amen.

December 9

"The Heart is Everything"

"At the center of care for the heart is the love of God. This must be the joyful aim of our life."

- Dallas Willard

O Come Let Us ADORE HIM

TODAY'S SCRIPTURE

When they had gone, an angel of the Lord appeared to Joseph in a dream. "Get up," he said, "take the child and his mother and escape to Egypt. Stay there until I tell you, for Herod is going to search for the child to kill him."

So he got up, took the child and his mother during the night and left for Egypt, where he stayed until the death of Herod. And so was fulfilled what the Lord had said through the prophet: "Out of Egypt I called my son."

When Herod realized that he had been outwitted by the Magi, he was furious, and he gave orders to kill all the boys in Bethlehem and its vicinity who were two years old and under, in accordance with the time he had learned from the Magi. Then what was said through the prophet Jeremiah was fulfilled:

> *"A voice is heard in Ramah,*
> *weeping and great mourning,*
> *Rachel weeping for her children*
> *and refusing to be comforted,*
> *because they are no more."*

MATTHEW 2:13-18

REFLECTION

A few days after my 41st birthday, I found myself in the emergency room. I had been experiencing chest pains off and on for a few weeks. It was a nagging pain, but in my mind, nothing too serious. However, since it was recurring, I decided to get it checked out. Upon arriving to the ER, the nurses immediately began running tests. The bloodwork indicated elevated numbers leading them to believe I had had a heart attack. From there, they admitted me to the hospital and quickly began running additional tests.

During this process, a nurse assured me they would get to the bottom my heart issue because in his words, "the heart is everything." Two days later they determined my heart was indeed okay, and I was able to go home, but the nurse's words stuck with me: "The heart is everything."

Herod's violent response to Jesus' birth haunts the Christmas story. While the Magi searched for Jesus to worship him, Herod searched for Jesus to kill him.

Words like "goodwill," "joy," "peace," and "merry" fill people's social media posts and Christmas cards this time of year. It is, after all, "the most wonderful time of the year." But remember that the story of Jesus' arrival includes parents mourning over their slain baby boys. For these parents, there is nothing joyful, peaceful, or merry about the first Christmas. Hobby Lobby doesn't carry signs decorated with verses from this part of the story.

Herod's jealousy, insecurity, and arrogance displayed in his murderous decision illuminates the Messiah's polarizing nature. Simeon cautioned Mary: "This child is destined to cause the falling and rising of many in Israel, and to be a sign that will be spoken against, so that the thoughts of many hearts will be revealed. And a sword will pierce your own soul too" (Luke 2:34-35).

Jesus revealed the "thoughts of many hearts," as Simeon said. Herod's heart, fully exposed, showed a man willing to do anything, and I mean anything, to keep his power and political might. Herod, knowing there was only one true throne, tried to ensure it remained occupied by him alone.

During Jesus' ministry, he continued to reveal people's hearts. Judas's heart was greedy, some of the Pharisees' hearts were hypocritical, Pilate's heart was fearful, Peter's heart was contrite, and Mary Magdalene's heart was worshipful. In these encounters with Jesus, some hearts surrendered to Him, while others doubted, denied, accused, and even yearned for His crucifixion.

The moments leading up to Jesus' crucifixion revealed the hearts of those in the crowd. Many shouted, "Crucify Him! Crucify Him!" Eventually, Jesus was nailed to the cross, humiliated and bloody; the crowds got their wish. Before He was a toddler, Herod wanted him dead. And then as an adult, the crowds cried out for this same fate. Mary's heart was pierced

O Come Let Us ADORE HIM

with a sword; the people wanted her innocent son to die.

You get to choose everyday how you will view and act toward Jesus. Just as in Jesus' time on earth, your present divine encounter with him will reveal your heart as well. Will you let Him be the Lord of your life, thus dictating how you talk and act? Will you choose to see others as He sees them? Will you let Him be the master of your time, treasure, and talent? How you respond to Jesus reveals the condition of your heart.

And remember, "The heart is everything."

QUESTIONS

1) If your spiritual heart were to undergo a heart scan today, what would it reveal?
2) What can you begin doing today to have a healthier heart?

PRAYER

Father, I ask you to create in me a pure heart. Thank you for forgiving my sins through the sacrificial death of Jesus. I know my only hope of having a clean heart before you is through the washing away of my sins through Jesus' death on the Cross. I am forever grateful for His loving sacrifice. I intend to approach this day with my heart set on things above...all to your glory! I love you, Lord. In Jesus' name, amen.

December 10

God With Us

"So God throws open the door of this world—and enters as a baby. As the most vulnerable imaginable. Because He wants unimaginable intimacy with you. What religion ever had a god that wanted such intimacy with us that He came with such vulnerability to us? What God ever came so tender we could touch Him? So fragile that we could break Him? So vulnerable that His bare, beating heart could be hurt? Only the One who loves you to death."

- Ann Voskamp

O Come Let Us **ADORE HIM**

TODAY'S SCRIPTURES

"The virgin will conceive and give birth to a son, and they will call him Immanuel" (which means "God with us").

MATTHEW 1:23

The Lord is my shepherd, I lack nothing.
He makes me lie down in green pastures,
he leads me beside quiet waters,
he refreshes my soul.
He guides me along the right paths
for his name's sake.
Even though I walk
through the darkest valley,
I will fear no evil,
for you are with me;
your rod and your staff,
they comfort me.

PSALM 23:1-4

Have I not commanded you? Be strong and courageous. Do not be afraid; do not be discouraged, for the Lord your God will be with you wherever you go.

JOSHUA 1:9

REFLECTION

With. It's a tiny, insignificant word. A basic preposition, neither a noun nor verb. A word mindlessly used. Would you like bacon *with* your eggs? Are you riding *with* her? I sat *with* my friends. I ate dinner *with* my family. "With" is not the sort of word we spend time meditating on. It's just a throw-away word. Or maybe not…

As Matthew records the story of Jesus' birth, he adds, "All this took place to fulfill what the Lord had said through the prophet: 'The virgin will conceive and give birth to a son, and they will call him Immanuel' (which means 'God with us')"

O Come Let Us ADORE HIM

(Matthew 1:22-23). Jesus is not only prophet, priest, and king, but Immanuel – God with us. In Jesus, God traveled from heaven to earth to be *with* us. Did you catch that? The God of the universe wants to be with us – seemingly small, insignificant humans.

And here is the thing: He is with us not only on the mountain when all is well, but He is also beside us in the valley when things are hard. Herein lies a truth that can be difficult to swallow: God being with us does not mean all hardships will be removed from our lives. In this broken world, sickness, relational struggles, financial difficulties, death, mental illness, terrible accidents, etc. remain part of life. However, knowing God is with us in those hardships means that they will not destroy us. In fact, God may use them to transform us.

Jane Eggleston's poem "It's in the Valleys that I Grow" shows the power of God being with us in the hardships.

> Sometimes life seems hard to bear,
> Full of sorrow, trouble, and woe,
> It's then I have to remember,
> That it's in the valleys I grow
>
> If I always stayed on the mountain top,
> And never experienced pain,
> I would never appreciate God's love,
> And would be living in vain
>
> I have so much to learn,
> And my growth is very slow,
> Sometimes I need the mountain tops,
> But it's in the valleys I grow
>
> I do not always understand,
> Why things happen as they do,
> But I am very sure of one thing,
> My Lord will see me through
> My little valleys are nothing,

O Come Let Us **ADORE HIM**

When I picture Christ on the cross,
He went through the valley of death,
His victory was Satan's loss

Forgive me Lord, for complaining,
When I'm feeling very low,
Just give me a gentle reminder,
That it's in the valley I grow

Continue to strengthen me Lord,
And use my life each day,
To share your love with others,
And help them find their way

Thank you for the valleys Lord,
For this one thing I know,
The mountain tops are glorious,
But it's in the valleys I grow!

I have been in a few valleys that challenged my faith. When I left for a college a thousand miles away from home, when my first girlfriend broke up with me, when the weight of ministry was bearing down on me, when my marriage was struggling, and when Sarah and I received some unexpected news in the hospital. At these moments, I felt helpless, lonely, heartbroken, confused, empty, and even ashamed. But thanks to the power and presence of Immanuel, the darkness, difficulty, and danger of those valleys were never the end. With God's help, I have walked out of those valleys (or maybe God carried me out?), a stronger person.

I am thankful for Immanuel who is always *with* us – on the mountaintop and in the valley. With Him, we know we will never be alone in the valley and, regardless of how terrifying or hard it is, it will not last forever.

So, the word "with" is not so insignificant after all. It is the bedrock of everything in life.

O Come Let Us ADORE HIM

QUESTIONS

1) Consider some of your own valley experiences. How does God's "with-ness" shape your perspective of these trials?
2) Is there anyone you know who is living through a valley right now? How could you show that you, too, are with them in this experience?

PRAYER

Heavenly Father, thank you for the gift of Immanuel — "God with us." Immanuel's arrival to earth clearly showed your desire to be present with humanity. You, Lord, put skin on to be with us. As I experience the valleys of life, keep in the forefront of my mind the truth that you are with me and shaping me during those times. Thank you, Immanuel. Amen.

DECEMBER 11

HE GETS US

"The incarnation reminds us that God is intimately familiar with our experience."

- TIMOTHY KELLER

O Come Let Us **ADORE HIM**

TODAY'S SCRIPTURE

"Come to me, all you who are weary and burdened, and I will give you rest. Take my yoke upon you and learn from me, for I am gentle and humble in heart, and you will find rest for your souls. For my yoke is easy and my burden is light."

MATTHEW 11:28-30

REFLECTION

A parent leaves work at 5pm. Driving home, she turns on a podcast and zones out, enjoying the detox time. She arrives at the house and heads inside. A mountain of dishes has formed in the sink. The kids' shoes are scattered in the hallway, and their backpacks are strewn across the kitchen floor. The dog is barking. The kids are fighting about whose turn it is to choose the TV show. Her husband is ready to talk about plans for the upcoming weekend, but she would rather not. Instead, she picks up her phone and begins mindlessly scrolling. Her husband follows suit.

One of the parents needs to take the oldest to practice. Someone needs to get dinner ready. Who is going to make sure the kids do their homework?

After dinner, the bedtime routine begins. Most nights, it is a minor miracle that no one is harmed in the process. Both parents look the other way when they see the pile of dirty clothes on the kid's floor. The last thing they want to deal with tonight is laundry.

Now that the kids are asleep (they only came out of their room twice tonight!), mom and dad know they should read, or do something productive, but instead they plop down on the couch and watch a TV show or scroll YouTube.

Crawling into bed they both feel exhausted, overwhelmed, anxious, and perhaps even ashamed. They wonder, *"How much longer can we do this?"*

You may have seen the commercials recently that conclude with the message *He Gets Us*. These commercials, highlighting the humanity of Jesus, creatively show how Jesus dealt with issues like poverty, hatred, betrayal, misunderstanding, and grief. The commercials emphasize that God understands us, including the daily struggles.

Two "He gets us" passages in the New Testament are in Hebrews. They read:

- "For this reason he had to be made like them, fully human in every way, in order that he might become a merciful and faithful high priest in service to God, and that he might make atonement for the sins of the people. Because he himself suffered when he was tempted, he is able to help those who are being tempted" (Hebrews 2:17-18).
- "For we do not have a high priest who is unable to empathize with our weaknesses, but we have one who has been tempted in every way, just as we are – yet he did not sin. Let us then approach God's throne of grace with confidence, so that we may receive mercy and find grace to help us in our time of need" (Hebrews 4:15-16).

These two passages describe Jesus as one who represents us before God as our merciful and righteous High Priest. They tell us that Jesus was "fully human," experiencing the same type of struggles and temptations we all face. Jesus is uniquely positioned to help us because, while He knows the lure of sin, He never succumbed to it. And, while experiencing betrayal, hunger, homelessness, grief, and torture, He maintained perfection. Therefore, He is the perfect High Priest, teacher, leader, and savior.

God, through Jesus, got up close and personal with humanity, therefore He understands what it is like to live under pressure, be tempted by Satan, and bear the weight of the world. He was the recipient of the worst pain that humanity could inflict on a man when He was killed on the Cross. That man, who endured so many trials, is here to help us, the writer of Hebrews says.

The commercials are on point: *He gets us.*

O Come Let Us **ADORE HIM**

Back to the parents wondering how long they can hang on.

If you find yourself identifying with them asking, "How much longer can I do this?" Remember, you are not alone. Jesus is there to help.

The writer of Hebrews wrote that we should "approach God's throne of grace with confidence, so that we may receive mercy and find grace to help us in our time of need" (4:16). The truth is, we can confidently give all of our struggles, anxiety, shame, and overwhelm to God. When we try to hide it, hold it in, or pretend it is not there, our joy, peace, and hope will be squeezed out of us. It is infinitely better to give it over to God.

God's throne is a "throne of grace," which means He will not judge, condemn, or dismiss us for what we bring to Him. He wants us to give everything over to Him and in return He will give us mercy and grace to help us in our time of need. God will make a way even if it seems impossible right now. He is fighting for us.

When you wake up tomorrow, much of your day will likely resemble your previous days. But perhaps your mindset can be different knowing that Jesus is with you and is providing you with grace to handle whatever comes your way.

Today, hear Jesus say to you…

"Come to me, all you who are weary and burdened, and I will give you rest. Take my yoke upon you and learn from me, for I am gentle and humble in heart, and you will find rest for your souls. For my yoke is easy and my burden is light" (Matthew 11:28-30).

He gets us. Give everything over to Him.

O Come Let Us **ADORE HIM**

QUESTIONS

1) How can you approach your day differently, knowing that Jesus is helping you with your temptations and struggles?
2) What are some struggles or temptations you can bring before God's throne of grace today?
3) How have you seen God provide you with grace and mercy in the past to help you navigate life's struggles?

PRAYER

Father, I confidently approach your throne of grace to thank you for providing me with a Savior who made the perfect and final sacrifice for my sins. I know I would be lost without Him. I ask that you provide grace and mercy to me in my time of need. Thank you for Jesus' willingness and ability to help me when I face temptations and struggles in this life. I find immense joy and confidence in knowing that I do not have to face this world alone. In Jesus' name, amen.

December 12

A Gift Fit for a King

"Christ says, 'Give me all. I don't want so much of your time, and so much of your money, and so much of your work: I want you'."

- C.S. Lewis

O Come Let Us ADORE HIM

TODAY'S SCRIPTURE

After Jesus was born in Bethlehem in Judea, during the time of King Herod, Magi from the east came to Jerusalem and asked, "Where is the one who has been born king of the Jews? We saw his star when it rose and have come to worship him."
When King Herod heard this he was disturbed, and all Jerusalem with him. When he had called together all the people's chief priests and teachers of the law, he asked them where the Messiah was to be born. "In Bethlehem in Judea," they replied, "for this is what the prophet has written:
"'But you, Bethlehem, in the land of Judah,
are by no means least among the rulers of Judah;
for out of you will come a ruler
who will shepherd my people Israel.'"
Then Herod called the Magi secretly and found out from them the exact time the star had appeared. He sent them to Bethlehem and said, "Go and search carefully for the child. As soon as you find him, report to me, so that I too may go and worship him."
After they had heard the king, they went on their way, and the star they had seen when it rose went ahead of them until it stopped over the place where the child was. When they saw the star, they were overjoyed. On coming to the house, they saw the child with his mother Mary, and they bowed down and worshiped him. Then they opened their treasures and presented him with gifts of gold, frankincense and myrrh. And having been warned in a dream not to go back to Herod, they returned to their country by another route.

MATTHEW 2:1-12

REFLECTION

What is a gift fit for a king?

The Magi gave Jesus gold, frankincense, and myrrh. These gifts may have carried symbolic meaning. Gold (a precious, valuable metal) represented royalty; frankincense (used as part of a recipe for incense placed on the Jewish altar) indicated Jesus' deity; and myrrh (a resin put on a corpse to cover the smell)

O Come Let Us ADORE HIM

foreshadowed Jesus' death and burial.

As the Magi bowed to Jesus and offered Him their gifts, what was going through Mary's mind? Was each gift an affirmation of the angel's message to her, that he truly was the "Son of the Most High" who will "sit on the throne of His father David"? Was Mary thinking, "Wow, these are random presents for a baby. Could you not have just gotten him a new baby bed?" Or maybe she was thinking about how grateful she was for the Magi helping them re-stock their supply of essential oils. Turning to Joseph, I wonder if he contemplated his new assignment to help raise a child who would elicit a response like he saw from the Magi. Surely, he felt pressure.

In this season of gift-giving, pause to reflect on this question: What is an appropriate gift to give Jesus? Now, we typically, and rightfully so, reflect on the gift Jesus is to us. "For God so loved the world that He gave His son..." (John 3:16). I can think of no better gift than Jesus himself. But let's turn it around for a moment. What can we offer to Jesus?

I am going to be a bit brave for a moment and share my unpopular opinion. I believe "The Little Drummer Boy," written by Katherine Kennicot Davis, is an amazing Christmas song that should be sung more this season, not less. I think it is a "Top 3" Christmas song, easily. I must admit it hurts when I see the meme: "Mary, exhausted, having gotten Jesus to sleep, is approached by a young man who thinks to himself: 'What this girl needs is a drum solo'." While I can see why some think it is cheesy because the word "pum" makes up half its lyrics, please allow me to share a defense of the song.

First, in case you do not remember the lyrics, here they are...

Come, they told me, pa rum pum pum pum
A newborn King to see, pa rum pum pum pum
Our finest gifts we bring, pa rum pum pum pum
To lay before the King, pa rum pum pum pum
Rum pum pum pum, rum pum pum pum.
So to honour Him, pa rum pum pum pum
When we come.

O Come Let Us **ADORE HIM**

Little baby, pa rum pum pum pum
I am a poor boy too, pa rum pum pum pum
I have no gift to bring, pa rum pum pum pum
That's fit to give a King, pa rum pum pum pum
Rum pum pum pum, rum pum pum pum.
Shall I play for you, pa rum pum pum pum
On my drum?

Mary nodded, pa rum pum pum pum
The ox and lamb kept time, pa rum pum pum pum
I played my drum for Him, pa rum pum pum pum
I played my best for Him, pa rum pum pum pum
Rum pum pum pum, rum pum pum pum.
Then He smiled at me, pa rum pum pum pum,
Me and my drum

It is important to approach this song with your imagination ready to work. "The Little Drummer Boy" invites us to the stable where we not only see a mother, a baby, animals, and a drummer boy, but ourselves before the newborn king.

Two lines stand out:

1) *'I have no gift to bring... that's fit to give a king'*. As the song-story unfolds, the boy's sentiment is one I believe we all share. Considering Jesus' royalty, what can we offer Him to convey our admiration in accordance to His majesty? We seem so small and insignificant compared to Him. He is the Holy Son of God, whereas we are merely humans who struggle with sin, doubt, and life's ups and downs.

2) *'Then He smiled at me... pa-rum pum pum pum.'* The boy played his drum for the King, which seems trivial at first glance. But Jesus responded to the boy's cadence with a smile as if to accept the gift. The miniscule gesture – pa-rum pum pum pum – brought a smile to Jesus' face. The boy gave what he could to Jesus, and Jesus gladly received it.

O Come Let Us ADORE HIM

This season, reflect on what you can bring to Jesus. Consider how you can offer your time, treasure, and talent to Him. As baby Jesus grew up into manhood, He clearly communicated what He wanted most: your heart.

There is a day coming when we will finally see Jesus face-to-face. When that glorious moment arrives, I believe that when He looks at each of us, He will smile at the gifts we bring… to lay before our King.

O Come Let Us **ADORE HIM**

QUESTIONS

1) How can you use your time, treasure, and talent for the King's purposes today?
2) What are specific ways you can show your devotion to Jesus this holiday season?

PRAYER

Heavenly Father, I want to give you and your Son my all today. You deserve nothing less than all that I am. You did not hold back when you gave your Son to the world as our Savior. Thank you. Help me live today with gratitude and appreciation for the gift of your Son. In Jesus' name, amen.

DECEMBER 13

WAITING AND WATCHING

"Do you remember those times as a kid when you could hardly sleep on Christmas Eve because you were so excited about opening presents in the morning? That anticipation showed that you had no doubt. We should have an even greater anticipation of Jesus. If you are not "eagerly waiting for Him" (Heb. 9:28), something is off. Ask God to restore hope in your life."

- FRANCIS CHAN

O Come Let Us ADORE HIM

TODAY'S SCRIPTURE

"But about that day or hour no one knows, not even the angels in heaven, nor the Son, but only the Father. Be on guard! Be alert! You do not know when that time will come. It's like a man going away: He leaves his house and puts his servants in charge, each with their assigned task, and tells the one at the door to keep watch.
"Therefore keep watch because you do not know when the owner of the house will come back—whether in the evening, or at midnight, or when the rooster crows, or at dawn. If he comes suddenly, do not let him find you sleeping. What I say to you, I say to everyone: 'Watch!'"

MARK 13:32-37

REFLECTION

Waiting is hard.

I am not good at waiting. I love a restaurant in town called Demos', but I rarely suggest it because I do not want to wait an hour to be seated. When I see a traffic light turn yellow, I usually stomp on the gas to avoid sitting at a red light. Waiting for the doctor to call with medical results? Excruciating. I strongly dislike waiting. I guess I have a "wait problem" (sorry for the dad joke). How about you? How do you feel about waiting?

Collectively, our culture struggles with waiting. We have designed an 'insta' world. You can buy your food using insta-cart, cook it with an insta-pot, then post a picture of it on instagram. Nowadays, we expect things to happen immediately…if not sooner!

There is an old Alabama song that captures how we, unfortunately, approach life. The chorus goes:

I'm in a hurry to get things done
Oh I rush and rush until life's no fun
All I really gotta do is live and die
But I'm in a hurry and don't know why.

Imagine living in first-century Jerusalem waiting for the

O Come Let Us ADORE HIM

Messiah. You know the prophets, like Isaiah and Jeremiah, preached that God would send a Messiah who would set everything right and restore peace to the world (see Isaiah 40-55). However, after hundreds of years of waiting, the Messiah has yet to come. And, as you wait, along with all of Israel, you witness wars, intense political strife, and debilitating Roman oppression. Over time, your once-strong faith weakens. You are exhausted by the wait; but still longing for the Messiah.

Of course, the day finally did come for the Messiah to arrive. In Bethlehem, the virgin Mary gave birth to Jesus, and an angel announced, "Today in the town of David a Savior has been born to you; he is the Messiah, the Lord" (Luke 2:10). The wait was over.

Jesus showed up, just as the prophets promised.

One of the saddest parts of the story is that after all that waiting, upon the Messiah's arrival, many in the community rejected him. John wrote, "He came to that which was his own, but his own did not receive him" (John 1:11). Heartbreaking, isn't it?

Today, we find ourselves waiting much like that early Jewish community. We live in the "in-between" – between Jesus' ascension and return, promise and fulfillment. Jesus, preparing His disciples for the "in-between" said: "Therefore keep watch because you do not know when the owner of the house will come back – whether in the evening, or at midnight, or when the rooster crows, or at dawn. If he comes suddenly, do not let him find you sleeping. What I say to you, I say to everyone: 'Watch'" (Mark 13:35-37)!

Jesus issues a warning for our wait: Stay awake! If we are not careful we can develop spiritual narcolepsy. Jesus, of course, is not talking about physical sleep, but the spiritual kind. This "in-between" we find ourselves living in can cause us to become apathetic, go the way of the world, lose our spiritual fervor, stop evangelizing, neglect the spiritual disciplines, or give up on attending church. Therefore, as we wait for His return, we must intentionally maintain our zeal and keep our spiritual eyes open, watching for His return.

O Come Let Us **ADORE HIM**

Waiting can be hard, but remember that Jesus' birth proves that God keeps His promises. Our wait includes an expiration date! When Jesus says He will return, we can count on it. And when He does, I think we will all agree that it was worth the wait.

In the meantime, we, like Israel longing for Immanuel's return, sing:

O come, O come, Immanuel,
and ransom captive Israel
that mourns in lonely exile here
until the Son of God appear.
Rejoice! Rejoice! Immanuel
shall come to you, O Israel.

O Come Let Us ADORE HIM

QUESTIONS

1) Are there ways you have been sleeping spiritually? If so, what will it require for you to wake up?
2) Do you know someone who is asleep spiritually? Is there something you can do today to help them wake up to God?
3) What are some ways today you can "keep watch" during the wait in order to be ready for Immanuel's return?

PRAYER

Father, you kept your promise to Israel by sending them a Messiah. Some were ready, some were not. You have promised to send your Son again to take us home. Help me remain spiritually awake and ready for His arrival. If there are areas in which I have been spiritually sleeping, please wake me up so I can live fully alive and alert for you today. In Jesus' name, amen.

December 14

"Who Among Us Will Celebrate Christmas Right?"

"Humility, the place of entire dependence on God, is the first duty and the highest virtue of the creature, and the root of every virtue. And so pride, or the loss of humility, is the root of every sin and evil."

- Andrew Murray

O Come Let Us ADORE HIM

TODAY'S SCRIPTURE

In your relationships with one another, have the same mindset as Christ Jesus:
Who, being in very nature God,
  did not consider equality with God something to be used to his own advantage;
rather, he made himself nothing
  by taking the very nature of a servant,
  being made in human likeness.
And being found in appearance as a man,
he humbled himself
  by becoming obedient to death—
  even death on a cross!

PHILIPPIANS 2:5-8

REFLECTION

Dietrich Bonhoeffer, while imprisoned in a Nazi concentration camp, asked, "Who among us will celebrate Christmas right?" It makes you wonder if there really is a "right" way to celebrate Christmas. Bonhoeffer continued, "Those who finally lay down all their power, honor and prestige, all their vanity, pride and self-will at the manger. Those who stand by the lowly and let God alone be exalted, those who see in the child in the manger the glory of God precisely in this lowliness."

Once, while at a conference in Los Angeles, I decided to take advantage of an opening in the schedule to check out Skid Row, which has a homeless population between 9,000-15,000 people. Until this point, I had only seen Skid Row in movies; I was ready to experience it firsthand. I got in my rental car and put my destination in the GPS.

I arrived as it was getting dark, and admittedly, I was a bit nervous. I wondered if doing this as a solo mission was a poor choice. But, as quickly as that thought came, I dismissed it. Upon exiting the highway, I immediately turned onto a street lined with tiny homes constructed of cardboard boxes, trash bags, and torn up blue and black tarps. I locked my doors and did my best to take in my surroundings. People sat on the sidewalks while others nonchalantly walked by. Nothing too alarming. However, I was amazed by the amount of makeshift cardboard and tarp houses. The area felt rundown and dirty, with graffiti covering its buildings like overgrown weeds taking over a garden.

Twenty minutes of meandering through Skid Row left me feeling adventurous, so I put Rodeo Drive in my smartphone's GPS. Next stop, Beverly Hills. When I arrived, I turned off the GPS and cruised slowly, letting my curiosity take the lead. As I ventured through each neighborhood, I took in the sights of the mansions, immaculate lawns, and luxury cars parked in the driveways. I passed one home that seemed to be hosting a party, with very well-dressed people standing in the driveway and on the sidewalk. Driving slowly, paparazzi style, I watched for a famous movie star, athlete, or other Hollywood icon.

In one hour, I was able to tour one of the poorest areas in the United States and one of the wealthiest, as they are separated by only thirteen miles.

If Jesus were born today, would His birthplace resemble more of a Beverly Hills mansion or a Skid Row tarp? Beverly Hills, ground zero for glitz, glamour, power, and prestige is a far cry from Skid Row's forgettable tent city lined with nobodies. Jesus was born in Bethlehem to a young down-to-earth couple in a down-to-earth village. While Jesus' birthplace was not exactly Skid Row, it was most certainly not Beverly Hills either. Jesus was born in a manger, not a mansion. Almost forgettable by human standards.

This Christmas, set your gaze on the one who came to earth through the lowliest of means. Despite the world's pressure to seek honor, prestige, and power, choose the humble mindset modeled by the one who "made himself nothing by taking the very nature of a servant, being made in human likeness" (Philippians 2:7). And keep in mind that although living humbly may not get you the glitz and glamour today, the heavenly home awaiting us will outshine even the best that Beverly Hills has to offer.

O Come Let Us **ADORE HIM**

Questions

1) Have pride, arrogance, or self-centeredness inhibited your ability to see God working in your life or in the lives of others? If so, what steps can you take today to rid yourself of those things?
2) How can you grow in humility today?

Prayer

Father, thank you for displaying your glory in the lowly, down-to-earth birth of your Son. Teach me, Lord, to be humble like your Son. Please remove any pride or self-centeredness from my heart. I want to live in full dependence on you; this world has nothing to offer that compares to you. I want to exalt you alone in my life today. You, alone, are worthy of my worship and adoration. In Jesus' name, amen.

December 15

Satan's Perspective on Christmas

"The Devil is vicious, but he's not victorious."

- Lysa TerKeurst

O Come Let Us ADORE HIM

TODAY'S SCRIPTURE

Be alert and of sober mind. Your enemy the devil prowls around like a roaring lion looking for someone to devour.

1 PETER 5:8

REFLECTION

Through all the wonder and joy of Jesus' birth, we know Satan lurks in the background. He must have hated what was happening in Bethlehem. As if they were playing chess, God made a colossal move by sending Jesus as a human. Without a doubt, Satan was scheming his next move even before the Magi reached Jerusalem.

If, regarding Jesus' birth, Satan were interviewed, I think it would go something like this:

Interviewer: What do you think of Jesus being born in an animal stall in Bethlehem?

Satan: On the surface, it seems like an odd choice. The King of kings lying in a bed of straw? But I know God's ways have deeper meanings. So, no, I'm not fond of it at all. A glitzy palace with lots of guards, jewels, and luxury like Buckingham Palace follows suit with royalty and would have created more space between Him and the commoners. But His lowly birth? Ugh! Now ordinary folks feel like they can approach him and relate to Him. I work hard to make God seem *un*relatable and *un*approachable so this really throws me off. The last thing I want is for people to know how badly God wants a close relationship with them.

You know what else I hate? It shows the humility of Jesus. He was born in a dirty feed trough! Jesus said He wants His followers to be humble, but instead of just preaching it, He actually did it himself. Knowing people are more apt to follow suit if it's modeled, that move gave Him more credibility, from the start. And it pains me to say, but it's worked with some. Humble Christians present a great danger to my mission in the world because God keeps using them to do His best work in the world. They rarely focus on themselves – with their finite resources and power – but instead focus on their Master with His infinite resources and power. Humility is the antithesis to my work; the more I can convince humans to be prideful and self-centered, the greater my stronghold in this world.

Interviewer: What are your thoughts on Mary?

Satan: Well of course God had to show off again with another miracle, choosing a virgin to be the mother of his Son. I was hopeful Mary's situation in life, her reputation and future, would have given her pause and made her angry and unwilling to serve. Doesn't she know what she gave up? I hate that Mary said "yes" to God. It's another hurdle to overcome because I know her trust inspires others to trust my enemy, God. Mary's willingness to submit to Him makes *her* my enemy too.

Interviewer: Shepherds and Magi visited Jesus after his birth. Any thoughts about those visitors?

Satan: I mean, I have to give God credit for His power. He orchestrated a star to lead the Magi to Jesus. Then there was the heavenly host that appeared before the shepherds. God knows what He's doing. The star and the angels really didn't surprise me, though. What bothers me most is that people keep telling their story year after year. I wince every time I hear parents tell their children about the shepherds and Magi. If people would stop telling the stories altogether, I could affect more change. Stories of faithful people inspire others to deeper faith, and that's why I try to divert the humans' attention to what I can control. People consumed with materials things, Black Friday deals, and the next best gadget don't have time to tell the stories, so I push that agenda. And if that doesn't work, I make them believe they are too busy to share.

Interviewer: Herod was clearly threatened by the birth of Jesus. What's your take on Herod?

Satan: Now that's a guy I can appreciate! He was just a man holding on to power. I don't know anyone who, after getting on top, wants to lose it. Do you? So, I don't blame him for trying to kill Jesus. I loved that part of history! But what really bothers me about Christians is that when they talk about Jesus' birth,

O Come Let Us **ADORE HIM**

they include Herod's involvement, too. I wish I could erase that part out of Matthew's account. Here's why: When Christians talk about Herod, I fear they realize that opposition might come. I can do better work when Christians naively believe that they will never face any resistance. Because when resistance does come - and I will ensure it does - they aren't quite as prepared for it. And since they're not prepared, they find it more difficult to face, so they're more likely to give up and walk away. That, my friend, is a victory for me.

Interviewer: Thank you for sharing your thoughts. As you know, many people take time each year to focus on the birth of Jesus, and there's a lot of talk about the Christians' joy during the Christmas season. How about you, what brings you the most joy during this season?

Satan: I love it when people focus more on stuff than people. I appreciate it when people have an opportunity to forgive loved ones, or at least re-connect, but choose not to. It's great to see people become so busy and stressed that they forget to rest in God. The more stressed, anxious, and exhausted humans are, the easier it is for me to get them to be ugly toward each other. But really, I love it when Christmas is over, because I do see more joy, celebration, fun, and love during December, so it's nice when it's over and people get back to normal, which makes my job a lot easier.

O Come Let Us **ADORE HIM**

QUESTIONS

1) How is it helpful to view the birth of Jesus from Satan's perspective?
2) Which one of Satan's responses stood out to you the most? Why?
3) Why does humility pose such a threat to Satan?

PRAYER

Father, I know Satan is alive and well and he is seeking people to devour. When I consider Jesus' birth from Satan's perspective it helps me to understand how much he hates it when your people humbly serve you. Please protect me from the enemy and keep me grounded in the Truth of your Word. Thank you for defeating Satan at the Cross and Resurrection of Jesus. Empower me to live victoriously in Him today. In Jesus' name, amen.

December 16

Trusting God Through Disappointment

"God is God. Because He is God. He is worthy of my trust and obedience. I will find rest nowhere but in His holy will that is unspeakably beyond my largest notions of what He is up to."

- Elizabeth Elliot

O Come Let Us ADORE HIM

TODAY'S SCRIPTURE

In the time of Herod king of Judea there was a priest named Zechariah, who belonged to the priestly division of Abijah; his wife Elizabeth was also a descendant of Aaron. Both of them were righteous in the sight of God, observing all the Lord's commands and decrees blamelessly. But they were childless because Elizabeth was not able to conceive, and they were both very old.

Once when Zechariah's division was on duty and he was serving as priest before God, he was chosen by lot, according to the custom of the priesthood, to go into the temple of the Lord and burn incense. And when the time for the burning of incense came, all the assembled worshipers were praying outside.

Then an angel of the Lord appeared to him, standing at the right side of the altar of incense. When Zechariah saw him, he was startled and was gripped with fear. But the angel said to him: "Do not be afraid, Zechariah; your prayer has been heard. Your wife Elizabeth will bear you a son, and you are to call him John. He will be a joy and delight to you, and many will rejoice because of his birth, for he will be great in the sight of the Lord. He is never to take wine or other fermented drink, and he will be filled with the Holy Spirit even before he is born. He will bring back many of the people of Israel to the Lord their God. And he will go on before the Lord, in the spirit and power of Elijah, to turn the hearts of the parents to their children and the disobedient to the wisdom of the righteous—to make ready a people prepared for the Lord."

Zechariah asked the angel, "How can I be sure of this? I am an old man and my wife is well along in years."

The angel said to him, "I am Gabriel. I stand in the presence of God, and I have been sent to speak to you and to tell you this good news. And now you will be silent and not able to speak until the day this happens, because you did not believe my words, which will come true at their appointed time."

Meanwhile, the people were waiting for Zechariah and wondering why he stayed so long in the temple. When he came out, he could not speak to them. They realized he had seen a vision in the temple, for he kept

O Come Let Us ADORE HIM

making signs to them but remained unable to speak. When his time of service was completed, he returned home.

After this his wife Elizabeth became pregnant and for five months remained in seclusion. "The Lord has done this for me," she said. "In these days he has shown his favor and taken away my disgrace among the people."

LUKE 1:5-25

REFLECTION

Zechariah and Elizabeth were "very old" (1:7) when they discovered Elizabeth was pregnant. Until this moment, they had been praying for a baby, but their prayers had gone unanswered.

The void loomed over them. Whether in the marketplace, visiting with friends, or worshiping at the temple, parents and children peppered the landscape. Their greatest desire was many others' reality and they had to live in the tension.

Elizabeth saw mothers holding babies, caressing their backs, and gently rocking them. She witnessed a mom smile as her toddler hurried up to her to give her a hug. Zechariah heard dads brag about their son's strength and how they would continue the family business. Both understood that the only hope for their family line's future was a child. Perhaps when Psalm 127 was read, a pit formed in their stomachs: "Children are a heritage from the Lord, offspring a reward from him. Like arrows in the hands of a warrior are children born in one's youth. Blessed is the man whose quiver is full of them" (Psalm 127:3-5). Did they think, "What did we do wrong?" Did they ask God, "Why have you not blessed us like you have done for others?"

Despite this disappointment, Luke tells us, "Both of them were righteous in the sight of God, observing all the Lord's commands and decrees blamelessly." They refused to view themselves as victims, letting bitterness take root within them. Instead, they persisted in serving the Lord.

This elderly couple teaches us: Stick with God even when He doesn't answer your prayers (at least in the way we want). You never know what God is ultimately doing. After becoming pregnant, Elizabeth said, "The Lord has done this for me. . .In these days he has shown his favor and taken away my disgrace among the people." Despite the years of unanswered prayers, when God finally provided them with a child, Elizabeth gave Him the credit. She could have cursed God, said something like, "Well, it's about time, Lord!" Instead, she simply acknowledged His divine work.

A variety of life circumstances can cause bitterness to germinate within us: Job loss, financial problems, divorce, health issues, or the passing of a family member. These challenges are real and can have devastating consequences. But when these circumstances come – and they will – Zechariah and Elizabeth can be our guides. They did not become bitter or quit on God.

Darrell Bock wrote, "Bitterness will yield the fruit of anger and frustration, sapping the joy from life. Trust and dependence will cause us to find fulfillment in ways we would not even have considered otherwise. For example, how many childless couples have made a life out of ministering to other children, either through service in the church or adopting a child who no longer had parents who cared? Sometimes a roadblock is not a dead end, but a fresh turn in the road."

The pregnant Elizabeth proclaimed, "The Lord has done this for me." Despite years of heartache, she wasted no time praising her God. Like Elizabeth, keep praying, keep serving, keep worshiping. You never know what God is orchestrating behind the scenes, but His timing will be exactly right.

O Come Let Us ADORE HIM

QUESTIONS

1) How have you handled the disappointments and challenges that have arisen over the last year?
2) What lessons do you learn from Elizabeth and Zechariah that can help you handle future difficult circumstances?

PRAYER

Righteous Father, even in the challenges and storms of life, I know you are incomparably glorious and good. There have been times where I have struggled to understand what you are doing in my life, but I know whereas my viewpoint is limited, you see and know all things. Help me to grip tightly to you, just like Zechariah and Elizabeth did, throughout the ups and downs. Thank you for always protecting me and providing for me. In Jesus' name, amen.

December 17

The Lord's Servant

"I believe Christians often perceive obedience to God as some test designed just to see if we're really committed to Him. But what if it's designed as God's way of giving us what's best for us?"

- Craig Groeschel

O Come Let Us **ADORE HIM**

Today's Scripture

In the sixth month of Elizabeth's pregnancy, God sent the angel Gabriel to Nazareth, a town in Galilee, to a virgin pledged to be married to a man named Joseph, a descendant of David. The virgin's name was Mary. The angel went to her and said, "Greetings, you who are highly favored! The Lord is with you."

Mary was greatly troubled at his words and wondered what kind of greeting this might be. But the angel said to her, "Do not be afraid, Mary; you have found favor with God. You will conceive and give birth to a son, and you are to call him Jesus. He will be great and will be called the Son of the Most High. The Lord God will give him the throne of his father David, and he will reign over Jacob's descendants forever; his kingdom will never end."

"How will this be," Mary asked the angel, "since I am a virgin?"

The angel answered, "The Holy Spirit will come on you, and the power of the Most High will overshadow you. So the holy one to be born will be called the Son of God. Even Elizabeth your relative is going to have a child in her old age, and she who was said to be unable to conceive is in her sixth month. For no word from God will ever fail."

"I am the Lord's servant," Mary answered. "May your word to me be fulfilled." Then the angel left her.

Luke 1:26-38

Reflection

What do you think of Mary's initial response to Gabriel? Would you, too, have been "troubled" by his presence? What a proclamation: "Greetings, you who are highly favored! The Lord is with you." This encounter is so wildly unexpected and abrupt. Mary, going about her business, meets an angel who speaks words to her that will radically change her life. Mary... this young, ordinary girl, living a basic life like her friends and family, was going to carry, deliver, and parent the Son of God.

If this happened today, Mary would probably get on Google to see what to do next. (How did we ever survive without Google?) But, of course, her search would come up empty because she is the first and only person ever called to give birth to the Son of God. This is unfamiliar territory; there is no playbook for this job.

The pressure and stress Mary must have felt in her motherly role!

While pregnant, Mary surely experienced loneliness, fear, perhaps even judgment from others. While some might have tried to empathize with her, no one could tell her, "I totally understand what you're going through." Certainly, people laughed at her, gossiped about her, and completely avoided her. The role of being the Messiah's mother was a party of exactly one.

After Gabriel told her she would become pregnant through the Holy Spirit, Mary humbly said, "I am the Lord's servant… may your word to me be fulfilled" (Luke 1:38). Have more tender and beautiful words ever been spoken? Mary obediently accepted God's call, even though it meant the potential loss of her reputation in the community, a radical shift in her future, the new pressure of being Jesus' mother, and so many unknowns that would come with her newly assigned role. Let this be a lesson for all of us: God's call may not make sense to us. It may sound too challenging or even absurd. But, if He calls us to it, He will be with us through it.

Immediately before Mary accepted God's call, Gabriel said, "For no word from God will ever fail." In the New King James Version that statement is translated: "For with God nothing will be impossible." Even if from a human perspective God's plan seems impossible, if He says it, it will happen. Can a virgin become the mother of the Messiah? If God says so, yes! Can God become a baby, lowering himself to be raised by human parents and experiencing life as a human? Yes!

Mary surrendered to God so His unfailing word would be fulfilled in her. Later Elizabeth said, "Blessed is she who has believed that the Lord would fulfill his promises to her" (1:45)!

Philip Yancey wrote that Mary "was the first person to accept Jesus on his own terms, regardless of the personal cost." In her humble surrendering, without a doubt, God saw her, understood her, and loved her. And that would be enough for Mary to faithfully fulfill God's call in her life.

Although you will not find Mary's name in the Hebrews 11 "Hall of Faith," I believe she is part of the cloud of witnesses surrounding us as we run our Christian race. She sees us when we feel misunderstood, scared, and lonely (she has been there before). And maybe she speaks some quiet words of encouragement to each of us. I imagine her saying something like: *Keep saying 'yes' to the Lord, even if it does not make sense or seems impossible, because He will make the seemingly impossible, possible. Don't believe me? Look at the baby I got to raise.*

O Come Let Us **ADORE HIM**

QUESTIONS

1) What are your reactions to Philip Yancey's quote, "Mary was the first person to accept Jesus on his own terms, regardless of the personal cost"? What do you learn about trust and obedience from Mary?
2) Recall a time in your past when you had to trust God through challenging circumstances. What did you learn about God through that experience? What did you learn about yourself?

PRAYER

Father, I am thankful for your servant Mary who shows me how to trust you deeply, even in challenging circumstances. Forgive me for those times I fail to trust you. I'm constantly tempted to try to control everything, taking matters into my own hands, instead of releasing everything over to you. Help me loosen my grip, surrender to you, and trust you fully every day of my life. You are faithful, good, and true. I trust you. Amen.

December 18

Blessed is She Who Has Believed

"Faith is not believing in my own unshakable belief. Faith is believing an unshakable God when everything in me trembles and quakes."

- Beth Moore

O Come Let Us **ADORE HIM**

TODAY'S SCRIPTURE

At that time Mary got ready and hurried to a town in the hill country of Judea, where she entered Zechariah's home and greeted Elizabeth. When Elizabeth heard Mary's greeting, the baby leaped in her womb, and Elizabeth was filled with the Holy Spirit. In a loud voice she exclaimed: "Blessed are you among women, and blessed is the child you will bear! But why am I so favored, that the mother of my Lord should come to me? As soon as the sound of your greeting reached my ears, the baby in my womb leaped for joy. Blessed is she who has believed that the Lord would fulfill his promises to her!"

LUKE 1:39-45

REFLECTION

After telling Mary she would be the mother of Jesus, the angel then told her that Elizabeth, her relative, would also have a baby. So, Mary rushed to Elizabeth's home, about eighty miles away. About six months earlier, when Elizabeth's husband, Zechariah, was at the temple, the angel told him that his son, John the Baptist, would, "go on before the Lord, in the spirit and power of Elijah, to turn the hearts of the parents to their children and the disobedient to the wisdom of the righteous— to make ready a people prepared for the Lord" (Luke 1:17).

As Mary greeted Elizabeth, her baby leapt in excitement. In adulthood, John the Baptist would humbly say, "He must increase, I must decrease" (John 3:30). He focused on making Jesus front and center. In this initial greeting, even before his eyes had seen the Judean sunlight, he responded to Jesus. John the Baptist exemplified how we all should live – pointing to Jesus.

We know Elizabeth was "very old" (see 1:7) at the time, while Mary was only between fourteen to sixteen years old. So, we see these two women – one an elderly woman, the other a teenage girl – sharing in the motherhood of central figures in God's redemptive plan. Elizabeth blessed Mary. Mary's world was turned upside down; therefore, Elizabeth's blessing must have filled her with assurance, calm, and peace when she felt nervous, bewildered, and anxious. I love the quote, "When I needed you the most, you gave me your very best." Elizabeth gave Mary her absolute best. We all need Elizabeths in our lives... those people we can go to in our time of need.

Elizabeth, with her gray hair, wrinkled face, weathered skin, said to the adolescent mother, "Why am I so favored, that the mother of my Lord should come to me?" Isn't that response amazing? Elizabeth saw herself as favored, or blessed, by Mary's visit. Elizabeth did not act entitled to a visit, instead she was humbled by it. Further, Elizabeth expressed that she knew exactly who Mary's son was. She knew her son, John the Baptist, was the forerunner for the Lord, Mary's son. Right before her eyes, God was fulfilling His promise to redeem His people; and her son, John, would prepare the people to receive the Messiah.

Mary stayed with Elizabeth for three months (Luke 1:56). This time together shielded Mary from some of Nazareth's "talk of the town" because of the timing of Mary's pregnancy. While staying at Elizabeth's home, Mary likely helped Elizabeth out, as she was both old and very pregnant.

One more thing: Elizabeth told Mary, "Blessed is she who has believed that the Lord would fulfill his promises to her!" Mary is a model of faith. She, along with Elizabeth, accepted the call to participate in God's plan despite the significant sacrifices it would require in her young life. Applying Mary's example to our own lives, we could paraphrase Elizabeth's statement this way, "Blessed are we when we believe that the Lord will fulfill His promises in us."

- Blessed are we when we choose to serve others instead of expecting others to serve us.
- Blessed are we when we choose to pray for our enemies instead of seeking revenge.
- Blessed are we when we choose to spend time reading the Bible and praying instead of mindlessly scrolling on our phones.
- Blessed are we when we choose to give our time,

treasure, and talent in service of the Lord instead of spending it on ourselves.
- Blessed are we when we choose to tell our friends and neighbors about Jesus, invite them to church, or think of ways to make their lives easier.
- Blessed are we when we choose to pray for others on a consistent basis, check on them, and speak encouraging words to them.
- Blessed are we when we choose to view our sufferings and struggles as opportunities to cling to God and grow in our faith.

These women teach us an important lesson: *Trusting in God leads to blessings from God.*

Two unexpected mothers – an old woman and a young virgin – supported each other in their surprise pregnancies. Oh, to be a fly on the wall for those conversations! Consider this: both sons died in their early thirties, fulfilling their God-given missions. But, before John and Jesus even entered the world, we see two mothers offering their bodies as the place for God to knit these sons together in the womb. Innumerable blessings came to the world through John and Jesus. In fact, Mary and Elizabeth would themselves be eternally blessed because of their sons' faithfulness. Faith precedes blessing, which is exactly what we see with these two remarkable mothers.

O Come Let Us ADORE HIM

QUESTIONS

1) What are your thoughts about the line "Trusting in God leads to blessings from God"? What are some specific ways over the last year that you demonstrated trust in God? What have been some blessings you have seen because of that trust?
2) Try to put yourself in the shoes of Mary and Elizabeth. What emotions might they have felt in this calling from God? How do you think you would have managed that responsibility?

PRAYER

Holy Father, thank you for being a faithful God who keeps all your promises. You are my rock and refuge; you are unshakable. If there is any unbelief within me, would you please help me overcome it by the guidance of the Holy Spirit. Lead me to deeper trust in you, and when your blessings come because of that trust, keep me from becoming prideful. Instead, help me to in humble gratitude give you all the glory. In Jesus' name, amen.

December 19

The World Turned Upside Down

"Instead, Christmas gives us courage to be honest about this world. The birth of the King of kings reminds us that the political powers of our world will be upended by the incarnated Kingdom of God. The visitation of angels to the shepherds gives the humble and overlooked confidence that God has not forgotten them. The escape to Egypt strengthens our resolve to care for the oppressed."

- Nate Pyle

O Come Let Us **ADORE HIM**

TODAY'S SCRIPTURE

And Mary said:
"My soul glorifies the Lord
and my spirit rejoices in God my Savior,
for he has been mindful
of the humble state of his servant.
From now on all generations will call me blessed,
for the Mighty One has done great things for me—
holy is his name.
His mercy extends to those who fear him,
from generation to generation.
He has performed mighty deeds with his arm;
he has scattered those who are proud in their inmost thoughts.
He has brought down rulers from their thrones
but has lifted up the humble.
He has filled the hungry with good things
but has sent the rich away empty.
He has helped his servant Israel,
remembering to be merciful
to Abraham and his descendants forever,
just as he promised our ancestors."

LUKE 1:46-55

REFLECTION

Mary arrives at Elizabeth's house, they greet one another, then Mary sings a song expressing God's activity in the world surrounding Jesus' arrival. Her song, referred to as the *Magnificat* (which is the first word of the Latin version of the song), praises God for sending the Messiah to Israel. Mary says that God "has helped his servant Israel, remembering to be merciful to Abraham and his descendants forever, just as he promised our ancestors" (Luke 1:54-55). Finally, after over four hundred years of waiting, Israel's king has come; a new day has dawned.

Mary glorifies God for using her to contribute to the Messiah's arrival. Mary is not selfishly boasting like a wide receiver dancing in the end zone after scoring a touchdown. Instead, she is humbly expressing her gratitude to God. Her heart is fixed on God, not herself. While Mary acknowledges that all generations will call her "blessed," she undoubtedly knows God's providence has made it possible. She is simply God's vessel used to accomplish his will.

In the musical *Hamilton*, the characters proudly sing "the world turned upside down" to signal the end of British rule following the American victory at Yorktown in 1781, the decisive battle of the Revolutionary War. Alexander Hamilton, played by Lin Manuel Miranda, points to the imminent upheaval of the old order of things following the Yorktown victory. For the Americans, this meant entry into fresh territory with independence and opportunity. Out with the old, in with the new. The world was turning upside down.

Echoes of "the world turned upside down" can be heard in Mary's lyrics. We read:

"He has performed mighty deeds with his arm;
he has scattered those who are proud in their inmost thoughts.
He has brought down rulers from their thrones
but has lifted up the humble.
He has filled the hungry with good things
but has sent the rich away empty" (Luke 1:51-53).

On the one hand, the proud have been "scattered," the rulers have been "brought down," and the rich have been "sent away empty," she sings. On the other hand, the humble have been "lifted up" and the hungry have been "filled with good things." God's heart and desire for the world, as the song says, is for the humble to be lifted and the hungry to be filled.

The kingdom, inaugurated through Jesus' arrival and prophesied about for hundreds of years (see Isaiah chapters 40-55), is not just for the elite. All are welcomed to it and blessed within it. Whether you are poor, unsure where your next meal will come from, or down and out, God extends His love and invites you into His kingdom. Jesus' compassion, mercy, and care for tax collectors, children, lepers, and people with diseases proves the inclusive nature of the Kingdom. Many in Jesus' time,

O Come Let Us ADORE HIM

including the religious elite, did not approve of who He served, but their opinion did not stop Him. He saw the invisible, remembered the forgotten, and touched the untouchable. Jesus stood at the center of the world turning it upside down.

Remember that Mary herself was not a Palestinian elite. She was merely a teenage girl from Nazareth. A commoner. In today's terms, she would not have been sitting in luxury boxes with CEOs and celebrities at the game, but up in the twenty-dollar nosebleed seats. So, when she sings of the humble being lifted, her perspective comes from personal experience.

The world's gravitational pull will try to make us live right-side up. But, right-side up is wrong. Join Mary in turning the world upside down. God wants us to be change makers. And it starts today by intentionally serving others.

This Christmas you can participate in turning the world upside down by…

- "Adopting" a family to buy gifts for
- Making cookies or other snacks or crafts and delivering them to shut-ins
- Singing Christmas carols at nursing homes
- Volunteering to serve meals
- Donating to a trusted charity
- Being intentionally present with family and friends as much as possible

Faithfully and consistently serving others may not cause instant change; however, over time, God will use our service to turn the world upside down as more people come to experience the love, truth, and joy of the Messiah.

O Come Let Us **ADORE HIM**

QUESTIONS

1) What do you learn about God from Mary's song? What do you learn about yourself from her song?
2) Consider the idea of "turning the world upside down." List specific ways you have seen Christians "turn the world upside down" through their service to others.

PRAYER

Heavenly Father, use me to help turn the world upside down for the Gospel. Give me eyes to see others as you see them. Use me as a change-maker in this world so that more people will know you, love you, and want to serve you. I want nothing more than for people who are lost, to be found in you. I confess that the gravitational pull of this world can be hard to resist. Therefore, keep me strong in you and your kingdom purposes in this world. In Jesus' name, amen.

December 20

Greatness in the Manger

"A great man is always willing to be little."

- Ralph Waldo Emerson

O Come Let Us ADORE HIM

TODAY'S SCRIPTURE

In those days Caesar Augustus issued a decree that a census should be taken of the entire Roman world. (This was the first census that took place while Quirinius was governor of Syria.) And everyone went to their own town to register.

So Joseph also went up from the town of Nazareth in Galilee to Judea, to Bethlehem the town of David, because he belonged to the house and line of David. He went there to register with Mary, who was pledged to be married to him and was expecting a child. While they were there, the time came for the baby to be born, and she gave birth to her firstborn, a son. She wrapped him in cloths and placed him in a manger, because there was no guest room available for them.

And there were shepherds living out in the fields nearby, keeping watch over their flocks at night. An angel of the Lord appeared to them, and the glory of the Lord shone around them, and they were terrified. But the angel said to them, "Do not be afraid. I bring you good news that will cause great joy for all the people. Today in the town of David a Savior has been born to you; he is the Messiah, the Lord. This will be a sign to you: You will find a baby wrapped in cloths and lying in a manger."

Suddenly a great company of the heavenly host appeared with the angel, praising God and saying,

"Glory to God in the highest heaven,
 and on earth peace to those on whom his favor rests."

When the angels had left them and gone into heaven, the shepherds said to one another, "Let's go to Bethlehem and see this thing that has happened, which the Lord has told us about."

So they hurried off and found Mary and Joseph, and the baby, who was lying in the manger. When they had seen him, they spread the word concerning what had been told them about this child, and all who heard it were amazed at what the shepherds said to them. But Mary treasured up all these things and pondered them in her heart. The shepherds returned, glorifying and praising God for all the things they had heard and seen, which were just as they had been told.

On the eighth day, when it was time to circumcise the child, he was named Jesus, the name the angel had given him before he was conceived.

LUKE 2:1-21

O Come Let Us ADORE HIM

REFLECTION

Today's Scripture reading includes Luke's description of the birth of the greatest person to ever walk this planet.

Jesus' birth was stunningly simple. Down-to-earth. Free of fanfare and luxury.

On May 6, 2023, England held the coronation for their new king, Charles III. It is estimated that ten million people in the United States watched the coronation on television. Twenty million in the United Kingdom watched. Who knows how many tuned in from around the world? The ceremony was full of pomp and pageantry, attended by numerous foreign dignitaries, and cost approximately 250 million pounds (equivalent to about $300 million in U.S. currency).

Although both Charles III's coronation and Jesus' birth involved a significant event in the life of royalty, there is no way to overstate the stark contrast between the circumstances. Whereas millions of viewers watched the coronation of Charles III, Mary gave birth in an animal stall of a small backwoods village "…because there was no guest room available for them." Joseph, Mary, and a handful of animals were the sole viewers of Jesus' birth story.

It was not dukes and duchesses that traveled to visit Jesus, but rather shepherds: down-to-earth, hard-working men. Their presence foreshadowing the type of kingdom this baby would establish. All people, both the elite *and* common folks, would be welcomed as kingdom citizens.

Jesus' birth shows us that one's greatness is not determined by their birth environment, social status, or the splendor surrounding them, but who they are in the eyes of God. Jesus became the King of Kings, regardless of His birthplace or what visitors showed up. His entrance into the world required no outside fanfare or force to prop Him up.

Nathan, a successful business leader, once told the story of his meeting with Truett Cathy, founder of Chick-fil-A. While in Atlanta for business, Nathan contacted Mr. Cathy's office to inquire about visiting. The office administrator, to Nathan's surprise, said Mr. Cathy would be happy with a visit and invited him to the CEO's office for the following day. Nathan made his way to the headquarters with a list of questions in tow, excited to inquire and learn from such a successful businessman. He was surprised when, upon arrival, he was led to Mr. Cathy's office and the CEO sat with Nathan and inquired about *his* family, career, and life. Nathan's questions never got answered because Mr. Cathy had shown such great interest in *him*. Despite his massive net worth and amazing business acumen, Mr. Cathy made it apparent to Nathan that he was humbly turning the spotlight away from himself.

We learn the important lesson from Jesus' birth, as well as from Truett Cathy's example, that humility is the pathway to greatness. Greatness does not come from the size of your bank account, your business accolades, your popularity, or the square footage of your home. *True greatness is the outcome of a humble heart.* The more humble we are before God, the greater we will be in His sight.

The Royal Family, even with their fame and fortune, share level ground with everyone else. If we want to be genuinely great – as God defines greatness – it will only because we exhibit humility before others.

Jesus said, "You know that the rulers of the Gentiles lord it over them, and their high officials exercise authority over them. Not so with you. Instead, whoever wants to become great among you must be your servant, and whoever wants to be first must be your slave—just as the Son of Man did not come to be served, but to serve, and to give his life as a ransom for many." (Matthew 20:25-28)

Go ahead and strive for greatness. Not greatness as the world defines it, but as Jesus both defines it and embodies it: humbly putting others before yourself.

O Come Let Us ADORE HIM

QUESTIONS

1) Why is humility such a difficult characteristic to develop?
2) What is one thing you can do today to help you grow in humility?

PRAYER

Father, help me to be humble as Jesus was humble. I want to be great in your eyes and on your terms. Please remove any pride from my heart. Help me to live my life in a way that is pleasing to you. Protect me, Lord, from getting caught up in the world's hunger for possessions, popularity, and prestige. May I live to exalt you alone. In Jesus' name, amen.

December 21

Hope in the Manger

"In some ways, Christians are homeless. Our true home is waiting for us, prepared by the Lord Jesus Christ."

- Billy Graham

O Come Let Us **ADORE HIM**

TODAY'S SCRIPTURES

"Do not let your hearts be troubled. You believe in God; believe also in me. My Father's house has many rooms; if that were not so, would I have told you that I am going there to prepare a place for you? And if I go and prepare a place for you, I will come back and take you to be with me that you also may be where I am. You know the way to the place where I am going.
Thomas said to him, "Lord, we don't know where you are going, so how can we know the way?"
Jesus answered, "I am the way and the truth and the life. No one comes to the Father except through me."

JOHN 14:1-6

"But our citizenship is in heaven. And we eagerly await a Savior from there, the Lord Jesus Christ, who, by the power that enables him to bring everything under his control, will transform our lowly bodies so that they will be like his glorious body."

PHILIPPIANS 3:20-21

REFLECTION

My grandpa on my dad's side passed away on December 21st and his funeral followed on Christmas Eve. It amazed me how many attended the service, considering it was a day most people set aside for holiday festivities. I felt the embrace and comfort of our loving church family as many adjusted their family's plans to be there. Their presence was a beautiful tribute to my grandpa and a source of encouragement for my family and me. I will forever treasure the outpouring of love we felt by our church family on that bitterly cold Christmas Eve.

He had been sick for some time, but we still prayed for his recovery. We hoped he would feel well enough to spend one more Christmas at home. But his time had come, and he took his final breath a few days before Christmas. During the service, Fred Edens, our preacher, said something that has stuck with me ever since. He turned to the family, and gently commented,

O Come Let Us ADORE HIM

"I know you were praying for Arthur to be able to go home by Christmas. Well, your prayers have been answered. He's home." Fred's words provided comfort and perspective amidst our grief. Grandpa Long was home for Christmas. God *had* answered our prayers.

Jesus made it possible for my grandpa to go home because He left his heavenly home and came to earth to die for the sins of humanity. In other words, Jesus' willingness to *leave* home created the path for us to *return* home. Regardless of where you spend Christmas this year, remember your true home is in the presence of the Father; and His Son, Jesus, offered Himself as a sacrifice to pave the way there.

This understanding of our true heavenly home connects with something Solomon said in Ecclesiastes 3:11. Referring to God, he said: "He has also set eternity in the human heart." God placed within all people a longing for something more. Something deeper. Something more eternal, as Solomon says. This life – what we are experiencing in the here and now - is not all there is.

Recently, while on vacation, my wife, Sarah and I were walking down the beach enjoying an idyllic scene: the water, a beautiful emerald green, the sand, soft beneath our feet, the air, warm and salty. It was picture perfect, but she shared that as much as she appreciated the moment, wanting to soak it in, she knew she could not capture it to its fullest depth. Experience has taught her that amazing moments will not last forever. In other words, the moment may have provided a foretaste of heaven, but it was not heaven itself. It was a "thin space": an occurrence when the line between heaven and earth seems razor thin. Regardless of the beauty and wonder of any earthly enjoyments, deep down we know and feel that they are temporary. Fleeting. Never providing complete satisfaction for our souls.

However, there is a day coming when the longing within us will finally be satisfied. On that day we will experience unimaginable beauty, peace, and glory. Our faith will be sight, and we will see our Savior face-to-face. All will be perfection. We will be home.

O Come Let Us **ADORE HIM**

May we never forget, however, that the road to our heavenly home was paved by Jesus, who lovingly left His heavenly home to endure betrayal, beatings, and a gruesome crucifixion to save us from sin, death, and hell; and then to rise from the grave on the third day. There is not a person today, nor has there ever been a person, who could find his or her way to an eternal home without Jesus. He came to earth not only to *show*, but to *provide*, the way home.

Whatever you are going through today, remember: the best is yet to come.

Follow Him home.

QUESTIONS

1) Think about the idea of Jesus leaving His home to come to earth, ultimately to die for humanity's sins. What sacrifices did Jesus make to fulfill God's plan? How does this impact your own faith?
2) What "thin spaces" have you experienced? What did you learn from those moments?
3) If we know we have a future heavenly home, how might that shape how we live in the present?

PRAYER

Loving Father, I'm overwhelmed by the thought of how much Jesus endured so that I could have a way home to you. By the Holy Spirit's guidance, help my future hope to shape how I live in the present. I'm thankful to be a citizen of heaven. I long to be home in your heavenly presence forever. In the meantime, keep me anchored in your mission and truth. In Jesus' name, amen.

December 22

Joy in the Manger

"Joy, which was the small publicity of the pagan, is the gigantic secret of the Christian."

- G.K. Chesterton

O Come Let Us **ADORE HIM**

TODAY'S SCRIPTURES

"But the angel said to them, 'Do not be afraid. I bring you good news that will cause great joy for all the people. Today in the town of David a Savior has been born to you; he is the Messiah, the Lord. This will be a sign to you: You will find a baby wrapped in cloths and lying in a manger.'"

LUKE 2:10-12

If you keep my commands, you will remain in my love, just as I have kept my Father's commands and remain in his love. I have told you this so that my joy may be in you and that your joy may be complete.

JOHN 15:10-11

"Be joyful in hope…"

ROMANS 12:12

REFLECTION

My friend Shannon exemplified joy more than any person I have ever known. He and his family were members of the congregation I served in Texas. Shannon lived the last ten-plus years of his life with Lou Gehrig's disease. Despite the difficulties of getting up and ready for the Sunday service, rarely did he miss. When I would say 'hi' to Shannon before the service, he would muster his strength and tell me to "Preach the Word."

A die-hard University of Texas fan, Shannon loved to boast about his beloved Longhorns, especially to my wife, Sarah, a lifelong fan of the Oklahoma Sooners, Texas' biggest rival. I enjoyed watching the (mostly) friendly banter.

Whenever I visited Shannon at home, he was joyful, upbeat, and humorous. Light filled his eyes. Although I visited Shannon to encourage him, I was the recipient of the greater encouragement.

I am sure Shannon had his struggles and complained occasionally. Who doesn't? But I never saw that side of him.

O Come Let Us ADORE HIM

Instead, what I saw was a man exuding joy as his physical body slowly shut down. In full transparency, if roles were reversed, I do not think I could have managed things so gracefully.

How did Shannon remain joyful while dealing with such a dreadful disease?

He trusted God. He knew that while his physical body was deteriorating, he would one day receive a new body – a glorious body – in the presence of the Lord. Shannon held tightly to the hope of heaven, and that hope produced joy.

Put differently: *When trust and hope are at the root, joy will be the fruit.*

Many circumstances in life can keep us from being joyful. Globally, there are catastrophic events happening all over our planet. On any given day, you can turn on the news to find political strife, wars, economic problems, and natural disasters flash across the screen. In fact, the media thrives with a steady stream of it, understanding that bad news generates higher TV ratings, page clicks, advertising, and social media attention. They have learned how to commodify fear and anxiety, because keeping their audiences fearful and anxious leads to bigger profits.

Hitting closer to home, most of us, at some point deal with financial issues, relational struggles, work problems, crammed calendars, friend drama, and/or health concerns. Even as you read this, you are likely enduring some sort of struggle. Considering all of life's challenges, it may be tempting to disappear to some remote island, away from everything and everyone. However, once we realize that that is probably not the most responsible thing to do, we must choose to face each day head on.

Kay Warren explained, "Joy is the settled assurance that God is in control of all the details of my life, the quiet confidence that ultimately everything is going to be all right, and the determined choice to praise God in all things." The phrases "settled assurance," "quiet confidence," and "determined choice" stick out in this definition. Each phrase indicates that a willful decision is included in making joy a reality. Joy is *choosing* to trust that God is who He claims to be and will do what He says He will do.

In other words: *When trust and hope are at the root, joy will be the fruit.*

Many of us are challenged by a variety of joy-stealers:

- *Comparison.* We measure ourselves against others, which distracts us from what God is doing in our lives. Comparison commonly leads to jealousy, resentment, and bitterness.
- *Ingratitude.* Failing to give God thanks often leads to feelings of discontent.
- *Anxiety.* We let our fears of the future steal the joy of the present. We may fixate on potential problems that will most likely never materialize.
- *Self-centeredness.* When we consistently focus on ourselves, we forfeit opportunities to enjoy life-giving relationships and to celebrate the successes of others.
- *Fear.* We refuse to take risks or allow ourselves to be vulnerable because of the potential for being hurt, wrong, or misunderstood.

When you notice your joy lacking, ask yourself:

- Am I spending my time doing things that will help build trust in God or fuel my fears and anxieties?
- What activities or habits have helped increase my joy in the past? What will it require for me to begin those habits/activities again?
- What things consistently steal my joy? What is a positive step I could take to counteract the effect of those joy stealers?

As you look at Jesus in the manger, remember that Jesus' birth shows that God keeps His promises and loves you so intensely that He sent His One and Only Son to be your Savior and King. There is not a single thing this world can throw at you to separate you from God's love (see Romans 8:31-39). Trust Him. Hold tightly to your hope in Him, because *when trust and hope are at the root, joy will be the fruit.*

O Come Let Us ADORE HIM

QUESTIONS

1) Do you know someone who is exceptionally joyful? What can you learn from their example?
2) What are some ways you can become a more joyful person in the coming year?
3) What brings you the most joy during Christmas? Why?

PRAYER

Father, thank you for the wonderful gift of Jesus. His arrival shows how much you love me and that you keep your promises. Help me to embrace your joy to the fullest — I know your joy is my strength. Thank you for people like Shannon, who, despite great challenges, maintain their joy because of their faith in you. Help me to be like that. In Jesus' name, amen.

December 23

The Gift in the Manger

"Remember that the happiest people are not those getting more, but those giving more."

- H. Jackson Brown, Jr.

O Come Let Us ADORE HIM

TODAY'S SCRIPTURES

For God so loved the world that he gave his one and only Son, that whoever believes in him shall not perish but have eternal life. For God did not send his Son into the world to condemn the world, but to save the world through him.

JOHN 3:16-17

Remember this: Whoever sows sparingly will also reap sparingly, and whoever sows generously will also reap generously.

2 CORINTHIANS 9:6

Command those who are rich in this present world not to be arrogant nor to put their hope in wealth, which is so uncertain, but to put their hope in God, who richly provides us with everything for our enjoyment. Command them to do good, to be rich in good deeds, and to be generous and willing to share. In this way they will lay up treasure for themselves as a firm foundation for the coming age, so that they may take hold of the life that is truly life.

1 TIMOTHY 6:17-19

REFLECTION

Do you remember what the night before Christmas was like when you were a kid?

I remember bursting with excitement for Christmas. It was the hardest night of the year to fall asleep. For months, I had anxiously awaited Christmas; now it was *almost* here. That night I would employ the classic strategy of an early bedtime, knowing that time goes faster when asleep. However, I found that strategy to be ineffective, as time passed at a snail's pace. Lying in bed, staring at the ceiling, I envisioned what presents awaited me on the other side of this painfully slow night. Typically, I managed to get a *few* hours of sleep, but by 5:30 am, I would jump out of bed, navigate my way to the living room, and take in the scene that every kid loves: Santa's deliveries under the tree. Seeing the bike, or baseball bat, drums, remote control car, or whatever it was that Santa delivered, would, without fail, bring me intense joy. In fact, one year I was so excited about my new scooter, I immediately took it out for a test run – in six inches of snow!

As enjoyable as those Christmas mornings were as a kid, I get more excited as a parent. I love watching my daughters' Christmas morning excitement. Their eyes light up with smiles stretching from ear-to-ear as they take in and inspect each new gift. I would not trade those moments for anything. Although, I would not mind if they waited until at least 7:00am to wake up.

The exchanging of gifts is part of what makes this season so special. We typically think hard about what to get our loved ones, knowing our gifts to them are an expression of our love. Receiving gifts from loved ones is wonderful, but it does not compare to the joy of watching a loved one open our gift to them.

Timothy Keller mentioned that exchanging gifts at Christmas is "profoundly appropriate because it gets at the theological heart of Christmas: *that Jesus Christ is the only human being who wasn't born but was given.*" As we gaze into the manger, we see the wonderful gift that God gave us. Jesus is the best gift anyone could ever receive because He is our Lord and Savior. He is the source of our hope.

By appreciating the enormity of God's gift of Jesus to us, the natural response is to, with a grateful heart, want to please Him in return. And one of the ways we can please Him is to emulate His generosity by giving to others. Paul wrote, "God loves a cheerful giver" (2 Corinthians 9:7b). As God has richly blessed us, especially by giving us His Son Jesus, we can bless others.

Remember that Jesus said, "It is more blessed to give than to receive" (Acts 20:35).

Not only do we please God when we give to others, but being generous has personal benefits as well. In Summer Allen's article entitled "The Science of Generosity," she explained that years of research has shown that generosity is associated with better overall health, more happiness, higher self-esteem, increased job satisfaction, healthier relationships, longer lasting romantic relationships, and even delayed mortality. Allen commented, "A host of studies have uncovered evidence that humans are biologically wired for generosity. Acting generously activates the same reward pathway that is activated by sex and food, a correlation that may help to explain why giving and helping feel good."

Knowing that God is a giver at heart, and humans were made in His image, it is no wonder why we are healthiest and happiest when we are being generous: when we are generous, we are aligning with how our Creator intended us to live.

Giving, of course, is not limited to money. We can be generous with our time, talents, and energy as well. You can probably think of a time when someone was generous toward you by helping with a project, listening to you share a struggle, or sharing an encouraging word. And I bet their generosity toward you left you feeling better.

Looking in the manger reminds us that we have been blessed beyond measure by the generous gift we behold. God is, indeed, an amazing gift-giver.

By understanding how amazingly blessed we have been by God, let's be amazingly generous toward others.

QUESTIONS

1) Other than Jesus, what is the best give you have ever received? What made that gift so special?
2) In the next year, how might you be able to grow in generosity?
3) Who is the most generous person you know? What lessons might you be able to learn from them to help you become more generous?

PRAYER

Holy Father, thank you for the gift of Jesus. Even though I was undeserving, you gave your Son so that I could be restored to you forever. He is my hope. Help keep my eyes on Him so that I can be more like Him – putting the needs of others above my own. Cleanse me from my selfishness, pride, and greed. Help me to be generous like you. In Jesus' name, amen.

DECEMBER 24

PEACE IN THE MANGER

"If God be our God, He will give us peace in trouble. When there is a storm without, He will make peace within. The world can create trouble in peace, but God can create peace in trouble."

- THOMAS WATSON

O Come Let Us **ADORE HIM**

Today's Scripture

Rejoice in the Lord always. I will say it again: Rejoice! Let your gentleness be evident to all. The Lord is near. Do not be anxious about anything, but in every situation, by prayer and petition, with thanksgiving, present your requests to God. And the peace of God, which transcends all understanding, will guard your hearts and your minds in Christ Jesus.

Philippians 4:4-7

Reflection

Many historical accounts suggest that the "Christmas Truce of 1914" began with British, Belgian, and French soldiers singing *Silent Night* from the trenches on a cold Christmas Eve during World War I. Hearing the singing, their German enemies laid down their rifles, stepped out of the trenches and joined them on the battlefield, not to fight, but to join their singing. Eventually the two opposing militaries began to mingle. Over the course of the next few days, together they sang more carols, exchanged gifts, showed off pictures of their families, and even kicked the soccer ball around. The peaceful interaction, involving about 100,000 troops, was a welcome break from the soldiers' daily reality of war.

In an account recorded by *Time* magazine, Graham Williams of the Fifth London Brigade described the event like this:

"First the Germans would sing one of their carols and then we would sing one of ours, until when we started up *O Come, All Ye Faithful* the Germans immediately joined in singing the same hymn to the *Lards Adeste Fideles*. And I thought, 'Well, this is really a most extraordinary thing – two nations both singing the same carol in the middle of a war.'"

I showed a YouTube video recounting the truce to one of my daughters. When it had finished, she asked, "Did they go back to fighting?" I said, "Yes." To which she aptly asked, "Why?" Good question. Most accounts indicate the truce lasted until New Year's Day, although in some areas the fighting resumed earlier than that. However, it is amazing that the truce happened at all. In the middle of an intense war, enemies who only days before had been firing at one another shared a moment of human connection.

The story of the Christmas Truce resonates so deeply because it taps into the almost-universally held desire for peace. The image of enemy soldiers dropping their weapons and singing in unison points to greater possibilities for this fractured world.

Upon Jesus' birth, the heavenly host announced: "Glory to God in the highest heaven, an on earth **peace** to those on whom his favor rests" (Luke 2:14, emphasis added). Seven hundred years before this, Isaiah prophesied, "For to us a child is born, to us a son is given, and the government will be on his shoulders. And he will be called Wonderful Counselor, Mighty God, Everlasting Father, **Prince of Peace.** Of the greatness of his government and **peace** there will be no end" (Isaiah 9:6-7a, emphasis added).

Jesus is the Prince of Peace, and His arrival meant peace to those who were favored by God. So, if Jesus, the Prince of Peace, established a peaceful kingdom, why does there continue to be such a *lack* of peace?

One word: Satan.

Paul penned these words: "Put on the full armor of God, so that you can take your stand against the devil's schemes. For our struggle is not against flesh and blood, but against the rulers, against the authorities, against the powers of this dark world and against the spiritual forces of evil in the heavenly realms" (Ephesians 6:11-12).

Until Jesus returns and God makes everything right in the new heaven and earth, the devil will continue to create conflict, deceive humanity, and generate turmoil. On this side of eternity, we will continue to witness wars and chaos because of the evil forces continuing to wreak havoc on our world. Satan is ultimately the culprit of the lack of peace in our world.

Jesus was well aware of Satan's schemes. While encouraging the disciples to conduct His mission even while facing hostility,

He said, "Peace I leave with you; my peace I give you. I do not give to you as the world gives. Do not let your hearts be troubled and do not be afraid" (John 14:27). He later said, "I have told you these things, so that in me you may have peace. In this world you will have trouble. But take heart! I have overcome the world" (John 16:33). Jesus knew the disciples would experience trouble in this world, but He gave them His peace to sustain them amid the world's troubles.

Two truths are evident here:
1. Jesus' peace is our peace.
2. Satan continues to cause trouble.

Whenever Christians are present, so is the peace of Christ. Wherever you go, Jesus' peace is with you. This is a life-changing truth. Satan's aim is to harm you, but with the Overcomer's peace within you, you can remain steadfast, courageous, and hopeful. And, each of us should strive to impress on others that peace is truly attainable in this troubled world through Jesus Christ.

We may not have much control over the world's ongoing wars and political strife, but what we *can do* is be peacemakers wherever God puts us today.

Here are seven ways you can allow Jesus' peace to grow and work within you:

- Ask God each day to give you the peace of Christ
- Daily surrender to God so that the Holy Spirit can produce the fruit of peace within you
- Refuse to gossip or use hurtful speech about others
- Forgive people and seek reconciliation with those with whom you have conflict
- Resist the temptation to argue, grumble, and complain
- Cast your anxieties on God
- Refuse to take revenge on someone who wrongs you

Making the world a more peaceful place starts with you. Let His peace be your peace.

O Come Let Us ADORE HIM

QUESTIONS

1) As you strive to be a peacemaker, are there any fractured relationships where you can take the initiative to help bring healthy reconciliation?
2) Go back and read the list of ways to allow Jesus' peace to grow within you. Which action(s) would bring more peace in your life and in your relationships? Which one do you struggle with the most?

PRAYER

God, thank you for making your peace a reality for me through Jesus Christ. By the Holy Spirit's power and guidance, help me to be a peacemaker in this world. As I navigate this world full of trouble and strife, help me remain steadfast and courageous for you. In Jesus' name, amen.

December 25

Love in the Manger

"God loves each of us as if there were only one of us."

- Augustine

O Come Let Us ADORE HIM

Today's Scriptures

"Dear friends, let us love one another, for love comes from God. Everyone who loves has been born of God and knows God. Whoever does not love does not know God, because God is love. This is how God showed his love among us: He sent his one and only Son into the world that we might live through him. This is love: not that we loved God, but that he loved us and sent his Son as an atoning sacrifice for our sins. Dear friends, since God so loved us, we also ought to love one another. No one has ever seen God; but if we love one another, God lives in us and his love is made complete in us."

1 John 4:7-12

Give thanks to the Lord, for he is good.
His love endures forever.
Give thanks to the God of gods.
His love endures forever.
Give thanks to the Lord of lords:
His love endures forever.
to him who alone does great wonders,
His love endures forever.

Psalm 136:1-4

Reflection

Let's begin with a quick word study. The Hebrew word or concept *hesed*, though never used in Matthew or Luke's birth narrative (the New Testament was written in Greek, not Hebrew), quietly hovers over Jesus' arrival. *Hesed*, most often translated as "mercy," "faithful love," or, "covenantal love," is the key word used in the Old Testament to signify God's approach to His people.

In the Old Testament, God's *hesed* for His people was constant, like a lighthouse shining out over the sea. When I read the Old Testament, I am continually amazed by God's patience and grace for His people. Repeatedly, His people messed up royally (just read the book of Judges!), yet God continued to lovingly welcome them back. Even when the Israelites failed to be faithful to Him, God remained faithful to them. In a nutshell, the story of the Old Testament is that God tenaciously pursues His chosen people and continuously reaffirms His commitment to bless and redeem them.

Matthew and Luke certainly understood how Jesus embodied God's faithful love. Centuries before, God had promised to send a King who would establish an eternal Kingdom; and sure enough, the promised Messiah arrived to fulfill that promise. In Bethlehem, Jesus became the focal point for how God's redemptive plan for His beloved children would unfold.

Why is this important for us to understand? God's *hesed* - His faithful love - is the foundation of our lives.

Last year, I made a job change. After 18 years of congregational ministry, I started working with a non-profit organization called Hope for Haiti's Children. While I am deeply grateful to be a part of a wonderful kingdom ministry focused on Haiti, the transition has been more challenging than expected.

Since full-time ministry was so core to my identity, I was not prepared for the shock of no longer filling that role. I realized quickly that I was experiencing an identity crisis. Much of the scaffolding that propped me up in ministry – preaching every Sunday, participating in leadership meetings, being recognized as "preacher," doing pastoral visitation and studies, receiving regular appreciation and validation for my service, and everything else involved with that role – was no longer part of my life. For months, I felt vulnerable and lonely in church. The change was hard. Now, please understand, I am happy with where God led me – I would not change a thing - however, the transition has been tougher than I imagined. There have been plenty of moments when I have been overcome with sadness, remorse, confusion, despair, and loneliness.

I share with you my struggle so that I can also tell you how thankful I am for the incarnation. God's arrival to Earth reminds me that He intensely loves me and holds me in His merciful grip.

O Come Let Us ADORE HIM

His *hesed* - His faithful love - reaches me in my darkest moments so that I am never alone in my struggles. His love is a *certainty* we can embrace as we deal with the *uncertainties* of life.

This may be a challenging season for you. Perhaps you are battling addiction, mourning the loss of a loved one, or saddened by the reality that you will no longer celebrate Christmas with someone who was special to you. Maybe you feel lonely, overwhelmed, or afraid. Maybe you have been dreading Christmas because it feels anything *but* joyful, magical, and bright.

Regardless of what you are going through, I pray that as you peer into the manger today, you will see the face of God's *hesed* – Jesus Christ. In Jesus, God's faithful, covenantal love came to Earth to redeem us and give us hope. Paul said that there is nothing in all creation that "can separate us from the love of God that is in Christ Jesus our Lord" (Romans 8:39).

Since my college days I have loved the song "Faithful Love," even though back then I did not realize it was about God's *hesed*. It has helped me get through many difficult days. I hope it will encourage you as well.

> *Faithful love flowing down from the thorn-covered crown*
> *Makes me whole, saves my soul*
> *Washes whiter than snow*
> *Faithful love calms each fear, reaches down, dries each tear*
> *Holds my hand when I can't stand on my own*
>
> *Faithful love is a friend just when hope seems to end*
> *Welcome face, sweet embrace*
> *Tender touch filled with grace*
> *Faithful love, endless power, living flame, Spirit's fire*
> *Burning bright in the night, guiding my way*
>
> *Faithful love*
> *From above*
> *Came to earth to show the Father's love*
> *And I'll never*

O Come Let Us ADORE HIM

Be the same
For I've seen faithful love face to face
And Jesus is His name

God's faithful love entered our world up close and personal in the birth of Jesus. At the manger, we see God's faithful love – His *hesed* – face to face.

I pray that you will feel safe and secure in His *hesed* today.

O Come Let Us **ADORE HIM**

QUESTIONS

1) How can fully embracing God's faithful love in your life impact how you live on a daily basis?
2) What other hymns or worship songs help you better understand the love and faithfulness of God?
3) If we know God loves us, why do we often struggle to internalize it? Why do we question God's love?

PRAYER

Faithful and loving Father, thank you for coming near us in the birth of your Son. The Incarnation helps me understand how deep and profound your love truly is for me. Help me keep my eyes focused on Jesus, so that your faithful love will forever be in the center of my life. And help me channel your love toward others today. In Jesus' name, amen.

DECEMBER 26

CHRIST BORN IN US

"If Christ lives in us, controlling our personalities, we will leave glorious marks on the lives we touch. Not because of our lovely characters, but because of His."

- EUGENIA PRICE

O Come Let Us ADORE HIM

TODAY'S SCRIPTURES

"I am the vine; you are the branches. If you remain in me and I in you, you will bear much fruit; apart from me you can do nothing."

JOHN 15:5

My dear children, for whom I am again in the pains of childbirth until Christ is formed in you.

GALATIANS 4:19

To them God has chosen to make known among the Gentiles the glorious riches of this mystery, which is Christ in you, the hope of glory.

COLOSSIANS 1:27

I pray that out of his glorious riches he may strengthen you with power through his Spirit in your inner being, so that Christ may dwell in your hearts through faith. And I pray that you, being rooted and established in love, may have power, together with all the Lord's holy people, to grasp how wide and long and high and deep is the love of Christ, and to know this love that surpasses knowledge—that you may be filled to the measure of all the fullness of God.

EPHESIANS 3:16-19

REFLECTION

My guess is that this month you heard, and possibly sang, the traditional Christmas song "Joy to the World." The song begins this way:

Joy to the world, the Lord is come
Let Earth receive her King
Let every heart prepare Him room
And Heaven and nature sing
And Heaven and nature sing
And Heaven, and Heaven, and nature sing.

I love the line, "Let every heart prepare Him room."

O Come Let Us ADORE HIM

With a similar sentiment, Oswald Chambers wrote, "Just as Our Lord came into human history from outside, so He must come into me from outside. *Have I allowed my personal human life to become a 'Bethlehem' for the Son of God?*"

Before welcoming our first child into the world, Sarah and I did what most expectant parents do… we readied the house. We made sure the nursery was just right, the fridge was stocked, and the house was spotless. I will never forget the look Sarah gave me when she glanced over and saw me vacuuming the couch. I learned later that we were "nesting." You would have thought we were preparing to host royalty.

Just as expectant parents practice "nesting," we should continually ensure our hearts remain open and welcome to Jesus. If your heart needs to declutter sin, ask God to cleanse you. If you have closed the door to Jesus, open it up to Him. If your heart has grown cold to Him, ask Him to warm it.

Christians are the dwelling place of Christ. He lives in us through the presence of the Holy Spirit. And the Holy Spirit does not passively reside within us like a lazy houseguest. Instead, He actively works to form us into a Jesus-shaped mold. That is Paul's point when he writes, "And we all, who with unveiled faces contemplate the Lord's glory, are being transformed into his image with ever-increasing glory, which comes from the Lord, who is the Spirit" (2 Corinthians 3:18).

With Jesus living in us through the Holy Spirit, we are to live solely for His purposes and glory. Our agendas and desires ought to serve Him and not the other way around.

Imagine Jesus is you for the next 24 hours. He wakes up in your bed, puts on your clothes, eats your breakfast, and drinks your coffee, drives your vehicle to the office while listening to your radio, greets your co-workers. He attends your staff meeting, manages your projects, shows up for your appointments. He takes your kids to soccer, does your dishes and laundry, converses with your spouse, watches your shows, falls asleep on your couch. Your day is His day.

How do you think that day would go? Would anything change? What would stay the same?

O Come Let Us **ADORE HIM**

Imagining Jesus living your day is a sobering exercise, isn't it? It is for me! Jesus is God Incarnate, while we are frail human beings. We know our weaknesses, limitations, and faults. However, if you are a Christian, because of God's grace and the presence of the Holy Spirit, Christ *is* dwelling in you. Therefore, God's desire is for your day, to be His.

When people see us, they should see Him. When we speak, they should hear Him. We are to be the hands and feet of Jesus.

Today, prepare Him room in your heart, and let this day be His.

O Come Let Us **ADORE HIM**

QUESTIONS

1) Is there anything cluttering your heart right now? What can you do to de-clutter?
2) How does it make you feel to think of yourself as the dwelling place of Jesus through the Holy Spirit?
3) Who do you know that looks like Jesus? More specifically, what characteristics of that person resemble Him?

PRAYER

Father, I am humbled and honored to know that Jesus dwells within me through the Holy Spirit. Help me to yield to Him daily so that He can shine brightly through me and receive all the glory. I know my relationship with you and the opportunity to be Jesus' dwelling place are only possible because of your grace and mercy. Thank you. In Jesus' name, amen.

December 27

Christ in Us: His Faithfulness

"God never said that they journey would be easy, but He did say that the arrival would be worthwhile."

- Max Lucado

O Come Let Us ADORE HIM

TODAY'S SCRIPTURE

Therefore, since we are surrounded by such a great cloud of witnesses, let us throw off everything that hinders and the sin that so easily entangles. And let us run with perseverance the race marked out for us, fixing our eyes on Jesus, the pioneer and perfecter of faith. For the joy set before him he endured the cross, scorning its shame, and sat down at the right hand of the throne of God. Consider him who endured such opposition from sinners, so that you will not grow weary and lose heart.

HEBREWS 12:1-3

REFLECTION

Just keep running!

Navigating life's challenges can be exhausting. The media bombards us with bad news. Health problems hamper us or our loved ones. Difficult relationships stress us out. Our busy schedules overwhelm us. If you are not currently dealing with hardship, just wait, as something will eventually hit. That is the nature of life on this side of heaven. Jesus said, "In this world you *will* have trouble" (John 16:33). It is not a matter of *if* you will have trouble, but *when*.

Despite our cultural situation differing significantly from that of the First Century, Hebrews 12:1-3 offers much needed encouragement for us today. The writer of Hebrews compares the Christian life to running a race. The first-century Christians faced severe pressure from their opponents, who persecuted them because of their devotion to Jesus. Although, at least in the United States, we are not persecuted, we do face a myriad of obstacles that can trip us up as we press forward in our own Christian race.

The writer advised us to fix our eyes on Jesus as we run the race. Focusing on Jesus can help us in two ways:

1) Jesus models perseverance. Jesus remained faithful to God's mission while enduring extreme hardship. In the face of a Roman execution, Jesus stayed the course, enduring the cross because of the "joy set before Him." Jesus displayed how to

O Come Let Us ADORE HIM

handle challenging circumstances with unflinching devotion. He marked out the course for the Christian race. When facing troubles, we can learn from Jesus' refusal to compromise or concede in His own race and apply it to ours.

2) Jesus' victory should inspire us. Jesus sits victoriously at the right hand of God. When Jesus rose from the dead, He conquered death for all believers. Jesus is the "perfecter" of our faith because through His death and resurrection, He ensured that our faith would result in reconciliation with God and eternal life. To see Jesus is to see victory! Therefore, we can confidently run our race knowing that victory has already been secured through the faithful work of Jesus. *By focusing on the joy of the finish line, we can endure the pain of the race.*

While reading, I occasionally flip to the end of the book to peek at what is upcoming. I usually skim a couple paragraphs and get a feel for the outcome, but nothing too in depth. I also glance at the final page number, and after some quick math, take note of how many pages are left in the book. I love knowing where the story is headed.

I often think about how nice it would be to flip to the next chapter of life to see what is in store. But, or course, that is not possible. Thankfully, Hebrews 12:1-3 clearly states where the Christian story is headed. The finish line is located with Jesus who is seated at the right hand of the Father in glory. Through Him, the race has already been won; the final chapter has been written. Our task is to keep running with the knowledge that unimaginable joy will one day be ours.

Whereas the Cross was intended to shame Jesus, He scorned it through His resurrection. Regardless of how humiliating and gruesome His crucifixion was, the agony it brought was short lived. Jesus, and life, got the last word. He walked out of the grave, conquering life's biggest enemy – death, destroying its sting for the people of God. For Christians, death is simply a turning of the page to the next – and best – chapter, where Jesus joyfully awaits our reunion with Him.

Recently, I was talking with a Haitian friend whose community is overcome with gang violence, a dysfunctional government, a hunger crisis, and crippling inflation. The struggles are a mountain towering over the Haitian people. They are suffering. When I asked my friend how he is coping, he simply said, "With God, we will be okay. He is our strength. I trust Him."

That is what it looks like to run the Christian race with faith and perseverance. The crisis in Haiti may appear insurmountable, but with Jesus, my friend and all the other Christians in Haiti "will be okay."

Regardless of what you are enduring today, just keep running! It is a promise: The finish line's reunion will make the difficulty of the run worth all the effort. With God, we will ALL be okay.

O Come Let Us ADORE HIM

Questions

1) Are you experiencing any challenges right now? If so, how can Jesus' example help you deal with those challenges?
2) What are some spiritual habits/disciplines you can do to help you maintain your focus on Jesus?
3) What things distract you from focusing on Jesus? How can you minimize the effect of those distractions as you run your race?
4) Who is part of your "great cloud of witnesses?"

Prayer

Father, I am thankful Jesus secured my victory by dying on the Cross and raising from the dead. I know He is the pioneer and perfecter of my faith. I trust Him. When I get distracted, taking my eyes off Him, help me regain my focus. Also, give me the strength and wisdom to throw off whatever it is that hinders me as I run. In Jesus' name, amen.

DECEMBER 28

CHRIST IN US: HIS COMPASSION

"Every act of kindness and compassion done by any man for his fellow Christian is done by Christ working within him."

- JULIAN OF NORWICH

O Come Let Us ADORE HIM

TODAY'S SCRIPTURE

A man with leprosy came to him and begged him on his knees, "If you are willing, you can make me clean."
Jesus was indignant. He reached out his hand and touched the man. "I am willing," he said. "Be clean!" Immediately the leprosy left him and he was cleansed.
Jesus sent him away at once with a strong warning: "See that you don't tell this to anyone. But go, show yourself to the priest and offer the sacrifices that Moses commanded for your cleansing, as a testimony to them." Instead he went out and began to talk freely, spreading the news. As a result, Jesus could no longer enter a town openly but stayed outside in lonely places. Yet the people still came to him from everywhere.

MARK 1:40-45

REFLECTION

A leper covered in sores begs for healing. There's desperation in his voice. His eyes are red and swollen. His hair is disheveled. His clothes are filthy. He is a broken man.

His is a miserable existence. He's commanded to shout, "UNCLEAN! UNCLEAN!" to inform others of his presence. Lonely and afraid, he weeps an endless stream of tears. Pain and discomfort are his unwelcome guests.

"If you are willing, you can make me clean," he said to Jesus. He knew Jesus' power.

Jesus was indignant (v. 41). Why?

Indignant means "feeling or showing anger or annoyance at what is perceived as unfair treatment" (Oxford Dictionary).

God created a perfect world with everything just how He wanted it. But then Adam and Eve disobeyed God by eating the fruit, and corruption infiltrated the world. While creation was still good, an unraveling began as corrupt forces disturbed God's good world. This corruption manifested itself in sin, war, famine, injustice, and disease… like leprosy.

Jesus was not angry with the man; *He was angry at the world's brokenness manifested in the man.*

Jesus countered the effects of the world's brokenness by healing him, and in doing so He exhibited how the world is *supposed to be*. Timothy Keller noted, "Christ's miracles were not the suspension of the natural order but the restoration of the natural order. They were a reminder of what once was prior to the fall and a preview of what will eventually be a universal reality once again--a world of peace and justice, without death, disease, or conflict."

Read that line again: "Christ's miracles were not the *suspension* of the natural order but the *restoration* of the natural order." In other words, leprosy was not part of God's natural order for the world. It wasn't an issue in the garden, and it will not be a problem in the new heaven and earth. Death, disease, conflict, and injustice disturb Jesus because they do not align with God's desire for His creation.

As you consider how you can be like Jesus, consider these questions:

- Does the brokenness, sin, and corrupt influences of the world cause you to be indignant like it did for Jesus? Put differently: Do the things that broke Jesus' heart break your heart?
- If so, what do you do about that indignation?

I recently attended an awards presentation for one of my daughters. Each class from her grade sat quietly on the gym floor. The parents watched from the bleachers. One of the special education classes joined them. Half-way through the presentation a student from the special education group began rolling frantically on the gym floor. Immediately, one of the teachers embraced the student, attempting to settle her down. The student responded by shoving and biting the teacher. In a split second, another teacher stepped in. She pulled the student off her co-teacher and led the student out of the gym.

What happened next amazed me. Unfazed, the teacher moved on and immediately began helping another student.

I am convinced I was witnessing the compassion of Jesus channeled through those teachers. The patience they displayed was nothing short of a miracle.

O Come Let Us **ADORE HIM**

However, I must admit, I felt myself becoming indignant. I looked at my daughter sitting with her classmates and thought, "She just as easily could have been the girl rolling frantically on the floor." I began to question God. "Why are some of the kids so different than the others? Why are there any disabilities in this world? Why do some parents have to endure that challenge while others don't? Why God? Why not us? Why them?"

Of course, it is beyond my ability to comprehend why certain things happen to people. The older I get, the more I realize how little I really understand.

But as I looked over at that teacher now consoling one of the younger students, I saw her compassion. And though I do not totally understand how God works, what I do know is she was being the hands and feet of Jesus. And when He is around, it is going to be okay.

I also know the day is coming when God will restore all things, and Eden's perfection will once again become the reality. I long for that day because diseases, disabilities, pain, heartache, depression, anxiety, war, hunger, injustice, and even death itself, will be eliminated forever!

In the meantime, to cultivate more compassion and empathy for our broken world, I encourage you to pray this prayer written by Francis of Assisi:

Lord, make me an instrument of your peace.
Where there is hatred, let me sow love;
where there is injury, pardon;
where there is doubt, faith;
where there is despair, hope;
where there is darkness, light;
and where there is sadness, joy.
O Divine Master, grant that I may not so much seek
to be consoled as to console;
to be understood as to understand;
to be loved as to love.
For it is in giving that we receive;
it is in pardoning that we are pardoned;
and it is in dying that we are born to eternal life.

QUESTIONS

1) What might be some opportunities for you to cultivate compassion this week?
2) When have you been a recipient of someone's compassion? How did that make you feel?
3) How would you describe the world's brokenness to a child? What lessons can we learn from God by looking at the brokenness of life?

PRAYER

Father, thank you for your compassion. You have healed me spiritually and given me eternal life through Jesus. Help me to be a channel of compassion to others. Help my heart to break for the same things that break your heart. In Jesus' name, amen.

December 29

Christ in Us: His Service

"The King of the universe became a servant. But we, often being servants, long to be kings."

- John Stott

O Come Let Us ADORE HIM

TODAY'S SCRIPTURE

It was just before the Passover Festival. Jesus knew that the hour had come for him to leave this world and go to the Father. Having loved his own who were in the world, he loved them to the end.

The evening meal was in progress, and the devil had already prompted Judas, the son of Simon Iscariot, to betray Jesus. Jesus knew that the Father had put all things under his power, and that he had come from God and was returning to God; so he got up from the meal, took off his outer clothing, and wrapped a towel around his waist. After that, he poured water into a basin and began to wash his disciples' feet, drying them with the towel that was wrapped around him.

When he had finished washing their feet, he put on his clothes and returned to his place. "Do you understand what I have done for you?" he asked them. "You call me 'Teacher' and 'Lord,' and rightly so, for that is what I am. Now that I, your Lord and Teacher, have washed your feet, you also should wash one another's feet. I have set you an example that you should do as I have done for you. Very truly I tell you, no servant is greater than his master, nor is a messenger greater than the one who sent him. Now that you know these things, you will be blessed if you do them."

JOHN 13:1-5, 12-17

REFLECTION

Have you ever wondered: "What's it like to be on the other side of me?"

Do people leave encouraged after speaking with you? Do others view you as trustworthy? As you approach people, are they glad to see you coming or are they like, "*Uh-oh here they come*"? Do others know you care? Do people view you as genuine and kind?

When Jesus washed the disciples' feet, He set an example for how to treat others. Which leads to the question, do those on the other side of you see someone striving to be like Jesus?

For a moment, place yourself on the other side of Jesus in the upper room. As you recline at the table with Peter,

Andrew, James, John, and the other disciples, you see Jesus stand up, wrap a towel around His waist, and pour water into a basin. From there, He begins to wash the feet of His disciples one-by-one. Now it is your turn. He kneels and gently holds one of your feet in His hand. As He begins to wipe it, you feel the cool towel rub against your skin.

He finishes, rises, and proceeds to his place at the table. It takes a minute to process what just occurred. You just experienced what it is like to be on the other side of Jesus. The King of kings, performing the task of the lowest household servant, just washed your feet.

Later Jesus said, *"You call me 'Teacher' and 'Lord,' and rightly so, for that is what I am. Now that I, your Lord and Teacher, have washed your feet, you also should wash one another's feet. I have set you an example that you should do as I have done for you"* (vv. 13-14).

What Jesus has done for you; you must now do for others.

Regardless of the number of degrees we earn, letters behind our name, or how fancy our office is, nobody outgrows the call to serve. Jesus, the glorious Messiah, humbly washed his disciples' feet. If the King is not above washing feet (even Judas's feet), neither are we.

You may be frustrated with what is happening in the world. And, of course, there is no shortage of problems. But the truth is, you have little or no control over many of the world's events. However, what you *do* have control over is how you spend your God-given time and energy. You can use that time and energy watching the news, complaining, and scrolling social media. You can use it to build up your own little kingdom or to binge-watch Netflix. You can use it to seek the applause of the world.

Or you can use it to serve.

Carl Henry wrote, "The early church didn't say, 'Look what the world is coming to!' They said, 'Look what has come into the world!'" In the hours before Jesus' crucifixion, Jesus did not pick up a sword, organize a rebellion, or ask others to serve Him, no, He picked up a towel and washed feet. A humble servant had come into the world. A servant, born in poverty, spending much of His life homeless, changed the world.

Let's continue to follow His example and show the world a better way. The way of humble service.

Like Jesus, pick up a towel today and start washing the feet of those on the other side of you.

O Come Let Us **ADORE HIM**

QUESTIONS

1) How has someone served you in the past? How did their act of service make you feel?
2) What practical ways you can serve others in the coming year?

PRAYER

Father, thank you for Jesus' example of service. Help me to serve others in the same way He served. If there is any pride in my heart keeping me from serving, please remove it. In Jesus' name, amen.

December 30

Christ in Us: His Surrender

"Oftentimes, the more we surrender to God, the greater our ability to see His hand in our life."

- Charles Stanley

O Come Let Us **ADORE HIM**

TODAY'S SCRIPTURE

Then Jesus went with his disciples to a place called Gethsemane, and he said to them, "Sit here while I go over there and pray." He took Peter and the two sons of Zebedee along with him, and he began to be sorrowful and troubled. Then he said to them, "My soul is overwhelmed with sorrow to the point of death. Stay here and keep watch with me."
Going a little farther, he fell with his face to the ground and prayed, "My Father, if it is possible, may this cup be taken from me. Yet not as I will, but as you will."
Then he returned to his disciples and found them sleeping. "Couldn't you men keep watch with me for one hour?" he asked Peter. "Watch and pray so that you will not fall into temptation. The spirit is willing, but the flesh is weak."
He went away a second time and prayed, "My Father, if it is not possible for this cup to be taken away unless I drink it, may your will be done."
When he came back, he again found them sleeping, because their eyes were heavy. So he left them and went away once more and prayed the third time, saying the same thing.
Then he returned to the disciples and said to them, "Are you still sleeping and resting? Look, the hour has come, and the Son of Man is delivered into the hands of sinners. Rise! Let us go! Here comes my betrayer!"

MATTHEW 26:36-46

REFLECTION

Three times in the garden of Gethsemane, Jesus prayed, "If it is possible, may this cup be taken from me." Jesus expressed anguish about His impending death on the Cross. Luke added that as Jesus prayed, "His sweat was like drops of blood falling to the ground" (22:44). After asking God to take His cup, Jesus then said, "Yet not as I will, but as you will," humbly surrendering to His Father's will.

Jesus modeled trust as He wrestled with His upcoming crucifixion. For many of us, surrendering to God can be a monumental challenge, primarily because it means relinquishing control. And most of us love control.

The desire for control manifests itself in many ways:
- We feel the need to be in charge.
- We worry about the future, knowing things could happen to disrupt our lives in significant ways.
- We struggle to empower, champion, or cheerlead others, fearing they will do better than us, or not do as well as us.
- We steer conversations back to ourselves because we love talking about ourselves.
- We try to perfect everything so that we impress others or at least not look weak.
- We compare ourselves to others, constantly assessing how we measure up.

We are imperfect people with struggles, insecurities, and inadequacies. That is normal. The thread of the world's brokenness is woven through all of us. *However, the more we learn to surrender to God – to let go of control and trust Him – the more peace, joy, contentment, and hope we will have.* Our loving God knows what He is doing.

Surrender is hard because we often believe we are the heroes of our stories, and those around us serve merely as the supporting cast. The plot chronicles *our* experiences, and everyone clamors to see *us*. The world revolves around *us*.

Of course, that could not be further from the truth. The fact is life is not about you or me. It is about God. He is the star, the hero, of the story.

Imagine boarding an airplane and instead of turning right to find your seat, you step left into the cockpit. You approach the pilot doing the pre-flight routine and mention to him that you will be flying the plane today. He can find a seat in coach if he would like. Seem bold? How often do we try to take the pilot's seat despite knowing we are inept to fly the plane?

Jesus put His life into His Father's hands. And if Jesus released control, so should we.

O Come Let Us **ADORE HIM**

If you find yourself maintaining a death grip on your life, struggling to trust God, I encourage you to reflect for a moment on Romans 8:31-39. As you read this passage consider these two questions:
- What promises are made in this passage?
- What can you do with those promises to help you release control?

What, then, shall we say in response to these things? If God is for us, who can be against us? He who did not spare his own Son, but gave him up for us all—how will he not also, along with him, graciously give us all things? Who will bring any charge against those whom God has chosen? It is God who justifies. Who then is the one who condemns? No one. Christ Jesus who died—more than that, who was raised to life—is at the right hand of God and is also interceding for us. Who shall separate us from the love of Christ? Shall trouble or hardship or persecution or famine or nakedness or danger or sword? As it is written:

"For your sake we face death all day long;
we are considered as sheep to be slaughtered."

No, in all these things we are more than conquerors through him who loved us. For I am convinced that neither death nor life, neither angels nor demons, neither the present nor the future, nor any powers, neither height nor depth, nor anything else in all creation, will be able to separate us from the love of God that is in Christ Jesus our Lord.

O Come Let Us **ADORE HIM**

QUESTIONS

1) What practical steps can you take to surrender to God?
2) Which of your friends could you ask to help you live a life of trust in God?

PRAYER

Father, I know you oversee the world with power, love, and wisdom. You created this world and are sustaining it as I pray to you now. I trust that you work all things for good for those who love you and are called to your holy purpose. In those moments where I struggle to let go, please, with the help of your Holy Spirit, loosen my grip. In Jesus' name, amen.

December 31

Christ in Us: His Grace

"Be a dispenser of God's grace."

- Jeff Simmons

O Come Let Us ADORE HIM

TODAY'S SCRIPTURE

I thank Christ Jesus our Lord, who has given me strength, that he considered me trustworthy, appointing me to his service. Even though I was once a blasphemer and a persecutor and a violent man, I was shown mercy because I acted in ignorance and unbelief. The grace of our Lord was poured out on me abundantly, along with the faith and love that are in Christ Jesus.

Here is a trustworthy saying that deserves full acceptance: Christ Jesus came into the world to save sinners—of whom I am the worst. But for that very reason I was shown mercy so that in me, the worst of sinners, Christ Jesus might display his immense patience as an example for those who would believe in him and receive eternal life. Now to the King eternal, immortal, invisible, the only God, be honor and glory for ever and ever. Amen.

1 TIMOTHY 1:12-17

REFLECTION

Today is New Year's Eve, which means the new year starts tomorrow. It's time for a fresh start. A clean slate. What changes do you plan to make for next year? What good habits from this past year will you bring into the new year? What bad habits will you leave behind?

The last month we have been reflecting on the significance of Jesus' arrival to earth. What happened in Bethlehem changed the world. And I hope it will change your life. Bob Goff commented: "If you find a God who gave up everything to come live with us and die for us so we could finally get a taste of grace, you'll want to give that grace to everyone you encounter."

What a powerful idea: If you have found grace in the manger, you will want to give that grace to everyone.

Not surprisingly, Jesus' grace was on full display during His public ministry. In fact, He was questioned often about the people He associated with. In Matthew 9, when Jesus ate with tax collectors and sinners, the Pharisees were led to ask,

O Come Let Us **ADORE HIM**

"Why does your teacher eat with tax collectors and sinners?" Jesus' grace toward others caught the attention of the religious folks of the day. His grace didn't stop there. He stood up for the woman caught in adultery when people were ready to kill her, and He called a tax collector to be part of the Twelve. Jesus' ministry was characterized by grace. And so, as we follow Jesus and allow the Holy Spirit to transform us, our lives should be characterized by grace as well.

In our dog-eat-dog world that rewards fierce competition, perfect performance, and excellence in every pursuit, grace can get lost. Sometimes it feels as if there is no time or energy to be gracious. Life is all business. It takes too much effort to foster deep compassion for others. So, relationships stay surface level.

I encourage you to be different. Be the one to ensure grace is front and center. When others withhold it, be the courageous one who extends it. Did someone wrong you? Respond with grace. Are you being too hard on yourself? Give yourself grace. Frustrated with friends and family? Lead with grace. Mad at yourself for your own mess ups? Forgive with grace.

Satan, the accuser, loves it when we focus on our shame and guilt. His greatest tactic is convincing us we're the only ones who have ever (you fill in the blank). So, ashamed of our sin, we hide. Then, hidden in the dark, our shame festers and we find ourselves in a lonely, shame-filled place. Satan loves the isolation and the pain, so he tells us lies to keep us in that place. God's grace, however, leads us to a pathway of healing. Whereas guilt and shame cripple us in the dark, the light of God's grace brings healing and wholeness.

This upcoming year, choose to be a grace-giver. Give the benefit of the doubt. When someone makes a mistake, do not respond by shaming them. If you make a mistake, offer a heartfelt apology. If you are holding a grudge, let it go. If you need to tell someone you forgive them, do it today. Let the cycle of grace start with you.

QUESTIONS

1) If there is someone you have not been as gracious toward as you ought to be, what can you do today to change that?
2) What specific actions can you take to be a grace-giver in the coming year?
3) List three benefits you have received because of God's grace.

PRAYER

Father, thank you for graciously giving the world the best gift in your Son, Jesus. Embolden me to be a grace-giver every day of my life as I remember the abundance of grace you have given me. It is because of your grace that I can live with hope. Thank you. In Jesus' name, amen.

Acknowledgements

This book was a team effort. Meredith Hutchens, thank you for your careful and thoughtful editing. Brandon Wagoner, thank you for formatting the book and your encouragement along the way. Jeremy Robertson and Kelly Tomasi, thanks for reading early drafts and providing insightful feedback in the early stages. Meredith Davenport, thank you for putting your creative skills to work in designing the cover. Alexis Wamble, thank you for helping to get the word out about the book. Sarah, thank you for your thoughtful insights, patience, and support. Really, I cannot say thank you enough. I love you. Adelyn and Audrey, thank you for being so patient with me. I owe you a game of *Alligator, Alligator* and some chocolate milkshakes. Oh yeah, Panera Bread, thank you for starting your Sip Club membership. While writing, I drank my money's worth of your coffee…and then some.

BIBLIOGRAPHY

Bock, Darrell. "Luke," *The NIV Application Commentary* (Grand Rapids: Zondervan, 1996).

Boring, Eugene. "Matthew," *The New Interpreter's Bible* (Nashville: Abingdon, 1994).

Chambers, Oswald. *My Utmost for His Highest* (Nashville: Discovery House Publishers, 1963).

Culpepper, Alan. "Luke," *The New Interpreter's Bible* (Nashville: Abingdon, 1995).

Keller, Timothy. *Hidden Christmas* (Hachette, UK: Hodder & Stoughton Ltd, 2018).

Packer, J.I. *Knowing God* (Downers Grove: IVP, 1973).

Phelps, Laura. "You are not the hero of your story." *Walking with Purpose.* https://walkingwithpurpose.com/you-are-not-the-hero-of-your-story/. September 2, 2018.

Wright, Tom. *Luke for Everyone* (Louisville: Westminster John Knox, 2004).

Wright, Tom. *Matthew for Everyone* (Louisville: Westminster John Knox, 2004).

Yancey, Phillip. *The Jesus I Never Knew* (Grand Rapids: Zondervan, 1995).

If you would like to learn more about Hope for Haiti's Children, scan the QR code or visit the website link below.

Hope for Haiti's Children

WWW.HOPEFORHAITISCHILDREN.ORG

About the Author

Rob Long works for Hope for Haiti's Children as the Development Director for the Southeast region. Before joining Hope for Haiti's Children, Rob served in congregational ministry for 18 years. He is passionate about helping people grow closer to Jesus. He loves to preach, teach, and connect with people over a good cup of coffee. He lives in Lebanon, Tennessee with his wife, Sarah, and their two daughters.